Relationships and Learning

Caring for children from birth to three

Anna Gillespie Edwards

The National Children's Bureau promotes the interests and well-being of all children and young people across every aspect of their lives. NCB advocates the participation of children and young people in all matters affecting them. NCB challenges disadvantage in childhood.

NCB achieves its mission by
- ensuring the views of children and young people are listened to and taken into account at all times
- playing an active role in policy development and advocacy
- undertaking high quality research and work from an evidence based perspective
- promoting multidisciplinary, cross-agency partnerships
- identifying, developing and promoting good practice
- disseminating information to professionals, policy makers, parents and children and young people.

NCB has adopted and works within the UN Convention on the Rights of the Child.

Peers Early Education Partnership (PEEP) is an early learning intervention which aims to improve the life chances of children in disadvantaged areas. Its purpose is to raise educational attainment, especially literacy, by supporting parents and carers of children from birth to four in their role as first educators.

Peers Early Education Partnership
The PEEP Centre
Peers School
Sandy Lane West
Littlemore
Oxford OX4 6JZ
Phone: 01865 395145
Fax: 01865 395140
info@peep.org.uk
www.peep.org.uk

For information about PEEP publications and training phone: 01865 779779

Published by National Children's Bureau Enterprises Ltd, the trading company for the National Children's Bureau, Registered Charity number 258825. 8 Wakley Street, London EC1V 7QE. Tel: 020 7843 6000

© National Children's Bureau, 2002
Published 2002

ISBN 1 900990 75 X

British Library Cataloguing in Publication Data
A catalogue record for this book is available from the British Library

Designed and typeset by Jeff Teader
Printed and bound by Page Bros, Norwich

CONTENTS

ACKNOWLEDGEMENTS

The careful work of many people has fed into the genesis of this book. I should like to gratefully acknowledge the work of Peter Elfer and Dorothy Selleck as the original researchers for the National Children's Bureau Early Childhood Unit. I have drawn not only upon their very detailed observations of children, but also upon a series of original reports of the project.

I would also like to thank the Esmée Fairbairn Charitable Trust for supporting the original work, Sally Whitaker for her contribution as Acting Director of the Early Childhood Unit and Sue Owen for her helpful comments as the new Director of the Unit. Thanks are also due to Bethany Rawles and Diane Reay in the National Children's Bureau Publications Department, along with Ann-Marie McAuliffe in the Early Childhood Unit.

I am delighted that this book is published as a partnership between PEEP and the National Children's Bureau. I should like to thank Rosie Roberts for reading the first draft and encouraging me to tackle 'The Babies' in the first place and my family for their love and support. I also want to acknowledge the contribution, direct and indirect, of all the staff at PEEP, and all the families we work with, to my developing thinking about how adults support very young children's learning.

FOREWORD

Gillian Pugh
Chief Executive, Coram Family
Formerly Director, Early Childhood Unit, NCB

I am very pleased to have been asked to write a short foreword to this excellent book. *Relationships and Learning: caring for children from birth to three* had its origins in an innovative study of children under three in day care settings, undertaken by Peter Elfer and Dorothy Selleck when we all worked at the Early Childhood Unit. Funded by the Esmee Fairbairn Foundation, the project involved the detailed observation of children in a range of day nurseries, and aimed to make recommendations about how to develop relationships between staff and children in group settings which would improve the learning environment for babies. Anna Gillespie Edwards, the author of this book, has drawn both on this original research as well as her own considerable experience as director of the pioneering PEEP project in Oxford.

In the five years since the study was completed there has been very considerable change in government policy and in levels of provision for children under three, and also in our understanding of the importance of the first three years of life. We now know from research, for example, how quickly the brain is developing during the first twelve months of life, and how susceptible it is to environmental influences. We also know that environmental stress has a negative effect not only on how the brain develops but also on how it functions, and this underlies our capacity to make and sustain relationships. Positive and nurturing relationships during their earliest years are critical to children's ability to make and sustain relationships later in life. The work of Bowlby and colleagues in the1950s on the central importance of children's early attachment to their parents and carers has been revisited, and the importance of these early attachments in helping children to develop a secure sense of self and emotional equilibrium has been underlined. Peter Elfer and Dorothy Selleck's initial research study has contributed to this growing awareness of the importance of security in relationships and stimulation in learning, both of them at the core of this book.

The research agenda has also contributed to the expansion of services for very young children. Although the majority of children who have benefited from the additional nursery places in the government's childcare strategy have to date been three and four olds, the number of children under three in day care continues to grow as increasing numbers of women return to work after the birth of their children. The introduction of the Sure Start initiative is also bringing considerable additional resources for parents and children under three in to more than 500 of the most deprived communities in the UK. With its emphasis on both supporting parents and enabling those who wish to do so to return to work, and on children's health and early development, the messages in this book will be of particular value to all involved in Sure Start schemes.

The curriculum guidance to support the *Foundation Stage* for children from three to six, has now been supplemented by a good practice framework for younger children. *Birth to Three Matters: a framework to support children in their earliest years* has been developed for the Department for Education and Skills by Lesley Abbott and colleagues at Manchester Metropolitan University and will be published later in 2002. *Relationships and Learning* will provide an excellent accompaniment to that framework. Readers will also be interested in a further publication on the key person approach – *A Key Person Approach in the Nursery: building relationships for quality provision* (Elfer, Selleck and Goldschmied, NEYN, 2002).

Relationships and Learning is based on well informed and careful observation of babies and toddlers, and on many years experience of working in day care settings. It sees the world through the eyes of young children, and recognises the interdependence of their emotional and social development with their cognitive growth and development. It will help practitioners and parents alike to be more responsive to children's needs and interests.

Gillian Pugh
July 2002

INTRODUCTION

This book about the care of children from birth to three offers a structure to support reflection and staff development. It is underpinned by a belief that the close observation of children opens up opportunities for understanding their needs, thoughts, feelings, and interests, and for supporting professional dialogue with colleagues and with parents. It highlights the importance of close one-to-one relationships with young children for fostering their self-esteem, well-being and their ability to learn.

Children's experiences of daycare are at the centre of this book. It arises from a research study undertaken in 1996-7 by Dorothy Selleck and Peter Elfer from the Early Childhood Unit of the National Children's Bureau and funded by the Esmée Fairbairn Charitable Trust. By observing fifteen children in fifteen different nurseries, from their arrival and separation from parents in the morning to their departure and reunion with parents in the evening, the researchers aimed to try to see the world from the child's point of view in order to understand their experiences.

Close observation of ordinary happenings and interactions in daycare nurseries can show us the ways in which young children try to communicate their needs, the ways in which adults respond and the potential for building enriching relationships. Hours of minute-by-minute observations were recorded which have provided the examples for this book. The full text of the child observations is available for further study on the NCB website: www.ncb.org.uk The children appear throughout the book in direct extracts from the researchers' observations, along with what staff said in interviews about their work.

Of course, adults always bring their own assumptions, ideas and feelings to their encounters with children. It matters very much how adults view the capabilities of the children in their care. In writing this book I am, of course, drawing upon my own experience as a teacher in a variety of early years settings and as a parent who has, over the years, used most types of professional care for her children. Most of all, I have drawn upon my work in Peers Early Education Partnership. (I am currently Director of the original programme, Peers PEEP.) Our shared experience of supporting parents and carers of children from birth to five in groups in the community, at home and in playgroups and nursery classes has shown me that, when adults become more aware of the value of their everyday interaction with children, there is enormous potential to support children's learning and, most important of all, their desire to learn. We have also found that, when adults learn about how they support children's learning, it can powerfully affect their own self-esteem and view of themselves as learners.

Children in this book are seen as active learners, who bring thought, reason and feeling to their encounters with their environment and with other people. They learn through playful exploration and through interaction with others, and seek to communicate and represent their thoughts. Their learning is supported by close relationships with adults who see them as active learners and who seek to understand and encourage their interests.

As relationships are fundamental to the happiness and growth of young children, three of the four sections are explicitly about relationships: those between children and adults, children and children, and adults with each other. The fourth section, 'Playing and learning', also emphasises the importance of interaction and relationships, and highlights the powerful role which adults (and other children) play in supporting children's learning.

All the sections of the framework are interdependent and could be considered in any order. It has been organised into sections because adults often find it useful to divide things up into chunks they can think about. Babies and young children, on the other hand, do not have compartments in their learning. They can learn as much, or more, from a nappy change with a 'tuned in' adult as from doing an 'educational' activity with someone who has not been able to get to know their individual needs and interests and ways of communicating. Any everyday activity can be educational in the broadest sense of helping someone to learn.

Each section of the framework has several elements, all of them divided into several points. Section A, 'Relationships: adult–child', examines the relationships between adults and children, in the context of accepting children's feelings, responding to children's expressions of affection, offering physical care, setting limits and respecting and valuing the differences between people. In the belief that in order to thrive, children need warm, committed care that recognises their individuality, a case is made for adopting the key person approach* in order to create possibilities for secure attachment relationships.

As children grow, they come to appreciate the opportunities offered by a group setting for enjoying relationships with a wider circle of others, and adults can support them as they gradually learn to manage their relationships with other people. Section B, 'Relationships: child–child', looks at how adults can support children's developing self-concept, their relationships with each other, their friendships and the joys and difficulties of participating in larger groups.

Section C, 'Relationships: adult–adult', examines children's sensitivity to the quality of the working relationships between staff, and between staff and parents. One of the most important relationships, from the very young child's point of view, is that between his parents and carers. When his parents and carers share their knowledge of him and their concern for his welfare, it becomes a true partnership. The child is held safely by both his parents and carers and is able to move confidently between them.

There is immense potential in the parent–staff relationship to support the child, by offering opportunities for continuity, complementarity, mutual respect and deepened understanding of the child as an individual, as part of a family with a particular cultural background and as an active learner with strong interests of his own. When such a partnership can be achieved, it leads to confidence all round: confident staff, confident parents and confident children.

The relationship thread also runs strongly through the final section, D, 'Playing and Learning'. This highlights the role of the adult in supporting young children's learning: offering opportunities, doing things together, talking, listening, recognising children's individual interests and achievements. It helps young children's learning enormously when adults observe their playing and exploring closely and get to know their individual interests and favourite play patterns (schemas*). They can then offer communication and conversation in both words and body language about what interests a particular child along with appropriate resources and opportunities to feed that interest. To help all children's playing and learning, adults can create a learning environment which is not only broad and inclusive but also responsive to individual children's interests and enthusiasms.

Adults also support children's developing language and literacy by getting to know individual children well, or 'tuning in', so that they can recognise and respond to their intentions, communications and representations. These may be in sound and gesture, movement or mark-making. Together with an enjoyment of stories, rhymes and songs – fostered by enthusiastic parents and carers – these early representations are the roots of later achievements in literacy.

Section D also includes adults' learning in its consideration of the learning environment. Adults, like children, thrive in an environment where personal relationships are good and where they are seen as capable learners with potential for personal and professional development. This section advocates support for practitioners' own reflection and learning, time for observation of children and of each other's practice, as well as opportunities for accreditation which recognises that learning. When staff reflect upon their own practice, the quality is greatly enhanced, along with the job satisfaction. When they become comfortable with being lifelong learners, they are also in a powerful position to model positive learning dispositions* to the children.

Daycare practitioners are often doing a difficult and profoundly responsible job under pressure. To date, it has not been well rewarded either in terms of pay or status, and training and support are often inadequate. It is striking that, of the 28 practitioners interviewed as part of the study, all of whom were working with children under three, only 13 had completed any formal training.

Some practitioners may find some of the framework elements challenging. This may be felt in terms of individual practice, but it may also raise many questions about

nursery organisation, priorities and assumptions, for instance, the priority given to:
● children's need for individual, committed care and the key person approach
● partnership with parents, and what that means in practice
● observing individual children closely and supporting their learning.

This book is intended to sow seeds and to offer a supportive framework for development. Much of the good practice reflected in the framework is evident in very many care settings for children from birth to three. The purpose of this book is to value and build on that good practice by making it explicit so it can be shared by everyone, for the benefit of all the children in care settings, and their families, and for the satisfaction of all the adults who work in them.

Note about gender – 'He' and 'she' have been used alternately throughout the book, in recognition of the equal worth of male and female children.

* Terms followed by an asterisk are defined in the Glossary at the end of this book.

WHO'S WHO?

Many children appear in the examples throughout this book. They have been drawn from the National Children's Bureau research study. Here is a list of the main children who appear, who were observed in their nurseries during the study, and their age at the time.

Name	Age in months
Louisa	6
Andrew	7
Kimberley	7
Sam	11
Seamus	11
Sarah	14
Emmanuel	15
Evie	16
David	21
Aisha	23
Ross	24
Georgia	31

Staff and parents were also interviewed, and some of what they said is included too. All the names have been changed to preserve their anonymity. In addition, there is a fictitious member of staff called Rachel, who appears in some scenarios which were specifically developed for this book.

Note on ages and stages

While there are recognisable stages in child development, individual children's rates of development vary enormously, and are rarely consistent across the board.

A FRAMEWORK TO SUPPORT CARING FOR CHILDREN FROM BIRTH TO THREE

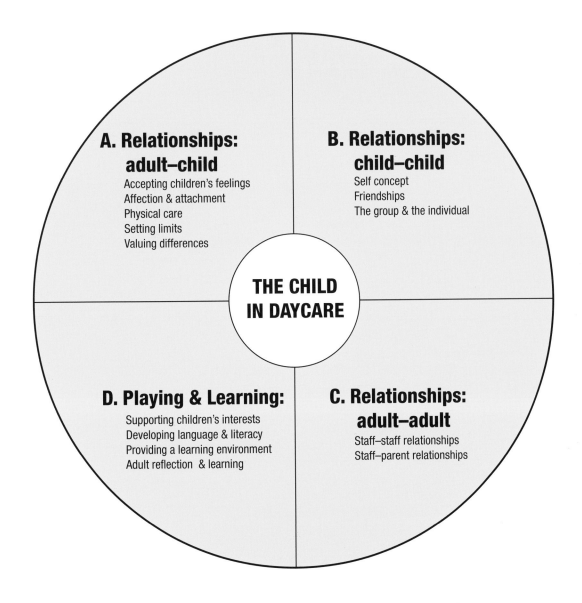

A. Relationships: adult–child
Accepting children's feelings
Affection & attachment
Physical care
Setting limits
Valuing differences

B. Relationships: child–child
Self concept
Friendships
The group & the individual

THE CHILD IN DAYCARE

D. Playing & Learning:
Supporting children's interests
Developing language & literacy
Providing a learning environment
Adult reflection & learning

C. Relationships: adult–adult
Staff–staff relationships
Staff–parent relationships

A. Relationships: adult–child

1 Accepting children's feelings

1 Adults accept children's emotional expressions, both positive and negative, and respond appropriately.
2 Adults acknowledge that 'unreasonable' behaviour is almost always reasonable from the point of view of the child.

2 Affection and attachment

1 Children's expressions of affection are responded to positively.
2 Children are cared for predominantly by one or two key persons and warm attachment is fostered.
3 Adults respond positively to children's expressions of attachment to their key persons.

3 Physical care

1 One or two key persons only carry out the tasks of feeding, dressing, nappy changing, helping children use the lavatory, giving medicine and settling them to sleep.
2 Physical care for the youngest children is personalised, being based on not only the child's physical needs, but also on sensitive observation of the child's emotional state and knowledge of her preferred routines.
3 Physical care is used as an opportunity for informal learning.

4 Setting limits

1 The limits set by adults are kept to the minimum, are consistent, and support the children's security and well-being
2 When adults set limits on children's behaviour, they explain them clearly but sympathetically.
3 The limits set allow for children's expressions of individuality and home routines and customs.

5 Valuing and respecting differences between people

1 There is a warm welcome for everyone entering the setting; adults actively value and respect the differences between people.
2 Staff form positive relationships with parents and take account of differences between families.
3 Discriminatory and judgemental behaviour and prejudiced attitudes are sensitively but clearly challenged.

B. Relationships: child–child

1 Self-concept

1. Adults acknowledge the importance of each child's developing self-concept and self-esteem, understanding the role of social interaction and adult expectations in their development.
2. Adults are aware of children when they are on their own and sometimes respond by actively leaving them in peace, whilst still remaining aware of them.

2 Friendships

1. Adults recognise and value children's developing friendships with one another.
2. Adults accept and encourage children's give-and-take games.
3. Adults enable children with shared interests and schemas* to enjoy playing together.

3 The group and the individual

1. Adults support children's growing capacity to participate in a group.
2. Adults understand and value the variety of ways in which children communicate and behave in groups.
3. Adults encourage and support children in accepting and valuing individual differences between people.

C. Relationships: adult–adult

1 Staff–staff relationships

1. Adults accept that young children are very sensitive to the feelings of the adults caring for them.
2. Adults model good humour, sensitivity and cooperation in their own relationships at work, acknowledging also when there are difficulties.

2 Staff–parent relationships

1. Staff acknowledge that all parents want the best for their children and support their choice to use daycare.
2. Staff actively establish positive relationships with parents and seek to work in partnership, finding out as much as they can about the children's family including other important adults, home languages, culture, religion, ethnicity, interests and achievements, etc.
3. Staff welcome parents and carers into the setting and share their practice and experience of the children freely with them.

D. playing and learning

1 Supporting children's interests	1 Adults support children's playful exploration of their environment, their ideas and their feelings. 2 Adults observe children's play carefully and seek to understand and develop their interests and schemas*. 3 Adults' responses are based on their knowledge of the child's interests and schemas*. Their conversations with children are matched to the child's interests.
2 Developing language and literacy	1 Adults recognise and support children's early communication and respond by adjusting their gestures, vocalisations and body movements to those of the child. 2 Adults appreciate the value of songs, rhymes, stories and humour and use them as part of their practice. 3 Adults support children's developing ability to represent their ideas and feelings in gesture, vocalisation, mark-making, construction and imaginative play.
3 Providing a learning environment	1 Planning, organisation and provision of play materials are developmentally appropriate and responsive to children's individual interests and needs. 2 Adults provide a learning environment that is broad, balanced and non-stereotypical, and which reflects positively the cultures and experiences of children's families and communities.
4 Adult reflection and learning	1 Adults take time to observe, reflect and revise their practice in a continuous cycle. 2 Adults are given and make good use of opportunities for accredited learning. 3 Adults model positive learning dispositions*.

A. RELATIONSHIPS: ADULT-CHILD

Introduction

This section is all about the relationships between adults and children in daycare and their great potential to enhance children's well-being and their learning. It contains five elements. Number one is about accepting children's feelings, particularly those underlying their 'unreasonable' behaviour. Number two is about affection and attachment, which all practitioners know play a vital role in supporting children's security and their ability to make the most of being in a nursery setting. This element in particular brings out the advantages of adopting a key person* approach to foster the commitment and continuity which supports young children's well-being. It also acknowledges some of the challenges.

Number three is about physical care: how practitioners personalise it and make the most of the opportunities it offers to develop closer relationships with individual children and for informal learning. Number four is about setting limits clearly but sympathetically, making sure they are kept to the minimum and support the children's security. Number five is about valuing diversity in a nursery: offering a warm welcome for everyone, being prepared to challenge judgemental behaviour and forming positive relationships with parents.

1. Accepting children's feelings

With a known and trusted adult, a child can feel safe to express both her affectionate feelings and her difficult feelings. How adults handle children's feelings, and the behaviour through which they express them, deeply affects the development of their self-esteem and confidence.

It is difficult to respond adequately to children's emotions without getting to know the children really well. Adults can get to know them well by making time for one-to-one interaction, and for observing them from a distance. Young children experience a great range of intensely-felt emotions, sometimes in a bewilderingly short space of time. Some of these emotions are much harder for adults to respond to constructively than others. Adults can ignore or reject children's feelings, or they can recognise them, accept them, offer shared celebration or comfort and, where appropriate, help them to move on.

When a child has developed an attachment to a key person*, this relationship provides an excellent context for a young child to try to make sense of her emotions. She may sometimes express anger and despair to her special person, just as she might to her parent, safe in the knowledge that she will not be rejected. In fact, a hot declaration in words or gesture of 'I hate you!' can be seen as the ultimate compliment!

As adults, we know how reassuring it is when we are going through a difficult time to know that someone who loves us is thinking of us. It also helps children to cope with their feelings if they know that their special person is holding them in mind, even if they cannot be with them at that moment. A trusting relationship like this can help children take the first steps on the long road to dealing with their own and other people's emotions.

Emmanuel's mother

Q: What happens when Emmanuel is tired or clingy when you bring him to nursery?

A: Well, staff talk to him – they are very gentle, talking to him. They don't just pull him off me – they stroke his brow and speak softly and then he normally just goes to them.

It is important to let children feel their difficult feelings, in this case, Emmanuel's inevitable sadness about being left by his mother. She knows staff are sympathetic with him, and don't try to brush his sadness way. This approach helps him deal with it and let his mother go, trusting that she will return at the end of the day.

Jacqueline

'If they are crying in the way of … getting it out of their system, I think it is really important they do that, and then my role is to let them do that and just be there for them.'

Jacqueline thinks it's important to let young children express their feelings and to 'be there for them'. Being there tells a child that you accept what she is feeling and are offering her a safe place to feel it.

1.1 Adults accept children's emotional expressions, both positive and negative, and respond appropriately

Babies experience and express a whole range of emotions, and they experience them very intensely. In the course of a long day in a childcare setting they may experience feelings of joy, love, sadness, grief, anger, anticipation, fear, wonder, contentment, bewilderment. Sometimes these feelings seem overwhelming, and as yet they have no words with which to begin to express them, or to gain understanding or comfort from others.

One- and two-year-olds are beginning to cope better, in that they can often wait a little longer for comfort, for instance. To do this they need to be able to hold the idea of their loved adult in their mind and trust that their needs will be met if they can just hang on! At about this age they may begin to experience complex emotions such as empathy and tenderness towards other children. But they are also subject to the fierce emotions of jealousy, revenge, aggression and the storms of rage and frustration called tantrums.

A first step is to get to know a child well and to observe her really carefully, particularly at key times such as when she is being left in the morning, or being picked up again. Babies cannot tell us how they are feeling in words. But careful observation will help carers spot the difference between a baby kicking in delight at being tickled and a squirm of discomfort or irritation.

A vital part of getting to know a child well is sharing knowledge with her parents. It helps a lot to know about any significant events, often changes, which are happening at home. After all, in the normal course of life young children face a lot of change and loss.

In practice, some feelings are easier for adults to accept and respond to adequately or appropriately than others. Tantrums are obviously a challenge to manage but, as we have seen, even children's positive emotions such as affection can produce complicated responses in adults (see A2 *Affection and attachment* on p. 18).

Sam's mother

'When he is distressed the staff acknowledge whatever's happened and then give him a cuddle – it's the same with me and my husband – as soon as it's been acknowledged, he's fine.'

Feelings are much more manageable when they are acknowledged. It is also very helpful for Sam that he gets a consistent approach at home and at nursery.

Lucinda about Emmanuel

'He's very independent, he'll let adults know what he wants. Sometimes I'll go over to him to give him a cuddle and he will just get up and walk away as if he doesn't want one and I'll think, "Okay, fine!"'

Part of being sensitive to children's feelings is respecting when they don't feel like a cuddle!

For understandable reasons, including the desire to protect their own feelings, adults – staff and parents alike – may seek to play down children's difficult emotions. They may try to cheer children up by singing jolly songs, jiggling them on their knee, or by seeking to distract them. The problem with this approach is that it denies the reality of the child's feeling and prevents her from dealing with it. In effect, it prevents her from even recognising the difficult feeling, which is an essential first step in learning how to manage it.

Denying a feeling expressed by a child conveys strongly to her that it is not acceptable, a 'no no'. This makes it even harder for her to deal with. As she has got a 'bad' feeling, she can feel that is 'bad' too, and that she will lose the love of her special person if she shows this dangerous feeling again. This is why well-intentioned remarks, such as 'Show us your happy face! We don't want that sad face, do we?', are not helpful.

Trusted adults can help a child recognise her feelings and offer her verbal language to name them. They can also help her contain her difficult feelings, through comfort and sympathy. Once the trusted adult has offered recognition, acceptance, sympathy and comfort, then they can help a child move on and get involved in something else.

There are many excellent picture books to share with babies and children that offer opportunities to think about feelings in a safe, enjoyable context.

KEYPOINTS

● Babies and very young children cannot tell us how they are feeling in words.

● It helps when adults accept children's feelings – especially the difficult ones.

● Trusted adults can help children recognise and learn to manage their feelings.

**Georgia (31 months)
with Marilyn**

Georgia … seems to be
scanning the room, the people
and the environment, for
something to create a drama
with. To begin with she
removes all the struts that
support the painting easel.
Marilyn notices and says, 'If
you do that it will fall down',
but Georgia continues to swing
it so that it will indeed fall down
… Marilyn comes over and sits
next to her on a chair and
unobtrusively replaces the
struts that support the easel,
while Georgia is vigorously
applying paint to the paper …
Marilyn is talking all the while to
Georgia, encouraging her,
being near her, talking to her
about what she is doing,
containing her aggressive
gestures.

*Marilyn knows Georgia very
well. She is aware that her
'unreasonable' behaviour is an
expression of her difficult
feelings, so she stays with her,
and by her presence and talk,
helps her to contain those
feelings. Marilyn stays calm in
the face of a storm.*

1.2 Adults acknowledge that 'unreasonable' behaviour is almost always reasonable from the point of view of the child

Often it feels unreasonable when children will not stop crying, or clinging, or go on 'whingeing' even when they have been given what they asked for. They may seem 'obsessed' with certain things, groundlessly jealous of other people or aggressive and destructive. Sometimes they refuse to do things which adults believe are necessary and for the child's own good. They may go on strike, for instance, refusing to accept a routine or rejecting food they have previously eaten with obvious enjoyment.

These kinds of 'unreasonable' behaviour are the same things which wind up parents at home, but in a nursery there are many added pressures – the sheer number of children needing attention, chores that need doing and sometimes tensions between staff members.

Being unable to stop a child crying can bring most adults to the point of despair. There are times when you just can't get it right, and both parent and professional feel that they *should* be able to.

However, if staff are given and take the time to stand back, observe and reflect upon a child's 'unreasonable' behaviour, it may be possible to see what lies at the root of it. It can help to remember that 'unreasonable' behaviour is almost always reasonable, or at least justified, from the point of view of the child doing it.

It is worth asking yourself 'Why?'. Why, when you have admired Zoë's painting and carefully written her name in the corner, did she immediately paint it out? Why is Dipak deliberately blocking the slide? Asking ourselves, 'What is that all about?' usually has a better result than asking a young child, 'Why did you have to do that?'

Much 'unreasonable' behaviour arises from children's difficult feelings. It is possible to accept and sympathise with these feelings, without having to allow what they want to do about it (see A4 *Setting limits* on p.31). Children very much need limits in order to feel safe. They need to begin to appreciate the needs of other people and start learning about rules of behaviour

Louisa (6 months) with Pete

Louisa has been crying inconsolably.
Pete says 'Oh, Louisa – It is a long day for you, isn't it ... ?'
Pete tries to see it from Louisa's point of view as a six-month-old baby, and offers sympathy, even though he is feeling rather worn down by her crying and has been wondering if it is his fault somehow.

Seamus (11 months) with Clare

... Seamus doesn't fight for a space on Clare's lap with his book but returns again to his bean bag and cuddles into it ... Clare strokes his back and his head, as he is lying on the bag. She leans down and talks gently and soothingly and whispers in his ear ... she has observed that Seamus doesn't find comfort in being held close, but seems to need the autonomy of self comfort and being next to her. Clare is Seamus' key person. She accepts his need to be quiet near her, but not on her lap. She has observed his behaviour and knows this is his preferred way of finding comfort.

which protect them. However, it helps when adults find responses to jealousy and aggression which do not also give the children the message that their feelings are either invisible, unmanageable or just plain bad.

Some unreasonable behaviour, such as winding up other children, can be ways of gaining attention. Adults may not want to give that attention – for fear of encouraging the unwanted behaviour – but is there a reason why a child needs extra attention?

Thinking about what underlies the behaviour reveals that some responses are inappropriate. Staff may want peace in the nursery, but insisting that two angry, hurt one-year olds kiss and say sorry will not achieve it in the long term, if the underlying problem is not resolved. Similarly, if children are distracted or guided away from a difficult task as soon as the going gets tough, they are deprived of the space to feel frustrated and they miss an opportunity to develop persistence, which is an important learning disposition*.

KEYPOINTS

● 'Unreasonable' behaviour almost always seems reasonable from the point of view of the child.
● It often arises from children's difficult feelings.
● Adults can accept these feelings without having to allow what children want to do about them.
● When thinking how to respond, it helps when adults ask themselves what lies behind the behaviour.

Conclusion

Young children need to know that their important adults accept their feelings, both positive and negative. They need to know that, while there are limits put on their behaviour to keep everyone safe, the full range of their feelings is acceptable.

Sometimes the emotional demands of a daycare setting full of children can seem insatiable and 'unreasonable' behaviour grabs adults' immediate attention. But it is not only the children clearly showing their emotions who need thinking about. What about the child who is 'no trouble' and who demands very little attention? What about the child who is neither clearly happy nor unhappy? Sometimes children's low-level distress can become invisible in a busy nursery. Practitioners can reflect together about how each child is experiencing their days in nursery and how they can support them.

QUESTIONS FOR REFLECTION

● Which of children's feelings are easier to accept and respond to?
● Which ones are harder?
● What kind of unreasonable behaviour do you find most difficult to deal with?
● Why might a one-year-old be needing extra attention? What can she do to make sure gets it? Is this the sort of attention she wants most?

2. Affection and attachment

Babies and very young children need warm, committed care and continuity. They exist most happily in relation to a small number of other people, with whom they seek to create intimate and intense relationships – relationships of attachment.

The framework in this book urges the adoption of the key person system*, in order that each child has someone (plus a back-up someone) in the nursery for whom they – and their family – are special. This person gets to know that child and her parents well, helps her to manage throughout the day, recognises her successes and understands her inevitable sadnesses and frustrations.

Real sociability comes through the experience of the reliable affection of a few close people (Goldschmied and Jackson, 1994). When young children consistently experience the feeling of being loved and looked after, they are enabled to reciprocate, offer affection, grow, explore and learn. They are then able to make the most of what is on offer in the nursery, including relationships with other people they know less well.

Ross (24 months) and Tess

Tess is watching from the window in the adjoining door in the playroom as Ross stirs and opens his eyes. He spots her at the window, jumps up with outstretched arms and runs to the door. Tess opens the door and embraces him warmly. He straddles her with his legs around her waist and they sit down together. Tess rubs the back of his head and strokes his back soothingly.

Ross has been asleep, and Tess has been keeping an eye on him through the glass door. She responds warmly and straight away to his greeting,

2.1 Children's expressions of affection are responded to positively

When children are given a positive response to expressions of affection, it helps them to feel safe, secure and remembered.

A very young child can be seen to be expressing affection when she calls or cries for an adult, smiles or laughs with them. She may seek an adult out, moving near to them, following them, putting her arms up to or holding on to them. Responding positively means reciprocating what the child has offered – returning the smile, the talk or the touch. Adults can also respond with affectionate holding, caressing and rocking.

Not responding positively means failing to notice a child's call, or noticing but declining to respond, for example, telling the child to go to another adult, turning *helping him reconnect with the world after his sleep.*

It is important for a young child to know they have someone for whom they are special. Just like Max in Maurice Sendak's Where the Wild Things Are *(1963), after an exciting time Ross wants to return to a safe place where he knows he is loved and will be cared for. In this well-loved children's story, Max has been wild and fierce and undertaken a big imaginary journey, but now he is tired and lonely and needs to be where someone loves him best of all.*

or moving away. It might mean turning down an invitation to join in a game or conversation or misunderstanding what the child is trying to express.

Adults may wonder what degree of response is necessary. Some children, after all, seem more needy than others. Is there such a thing as a 'good enough' response? Do adults need to be available to the children all the time, or just some of the time?

There are many demands on staff time, often conflicting, but even very brief responses from adults, such as smiling, eye contact across a room, a brief greeting or a touch can be as effective in helping children feel safe, secure and remembered as longer interchanges. It also helps when adults are careful to let children know when they have to go, at the end of a shift, for example, and remember to say goodbye, making sure they get eye contact and that the child understands they are leaving.

It is worth reflecting upon our own reactions to individual children. For a variety of reasons, some of them perhaps unconscious, we find some children much easier to be affectionate with than others. A professional awareness of the importance of responding positively to each child's expressions of affection can help practitioners meet the needs of all the children in their care.

Some children are able to ask for the affection they need in nursery. Others are less disposed to do this. It is especially important that these children experience relationships with adults outside their immediate family who offer affection as well as responding to the children's expressions of it. Both children and adults can learn to take the risk of offering and asking for affection.

Even if all a child's expressions of affection are responded to positively, they can still have a bad day at nursery. Many factors affect a child's well-being. However, a lack of response or a negative response certainly undermines a child's security and their ability to make the most of the nursery environment.

KEYPOINTS

● Babies and very young children need warm, committed care and continuity.

● Even a brief smile from a known and trusted adult can help children feel safe, secure and remembered.

Andrew (7 months) with Jan
Andrew is then put on the floor with the treasure basket* and picks up a metal sieve. Jan is now at the sink tidying up the bottles and calls across to him, in a singsong voice, 'Andrew, Andrew!'. Andrew is playing with the top of his sock, then he mouths the metal sieve, then he bangs it down on a tin and all the while he is watching Jan with another baby …

Andrew has become attached to Jan. She uses his name to re-establish her connection with him and maintain their thread of attachment. Calling out, like keeping eye contact, is one way of making sure a young child knows he is held in mind, even if for practical reasons, he cannot be held physically. Without this, Andrew probably would not have been able to enjoy exploring his sock and the sieve (note he still keeps his eye on Jan). At other times Andrew will need more sustained and intense togetherness with Jan.

2.2 Children are cared for predominantly by one or two key persons*, and warm attachment is fostered

Babies and young children need and actively seek to create affectionate and intimate relationships – relationships of attachment. Attachment relationships are characterised by feelings of love and affection and also by a sense of commitment. They offer young children a feeling of belonging, security and reliability. At home, of course, a young child's key attachment relationship will be with the family member who looks after her most.

In a daycare context, it is much easier to meet young children's need for warm, committed care and continuity if they are cared for predominantly by one or two key persons, rather than by the full range of the staff team. A child in a daycare setting has been left by the parent – her main attachment relationship – to be cared for by others. In this situation, it is immensely reassuring for the child to know that she has a special person who knows her and her family, cares about her and will reliably respond to her needs.

Having a key person, to whom she has a real attachment, can ease a child's inevitable pain on being separated from her parent and form a secure bridge into the different world of daycare.

If a child's key person forms a positive relationship with her parent, it can form the cornerstone of a partnership between nursery and home (see C2, *Staff–parent relationships* on p.67). This relationship can build trust and deepen not only the key person's knowledge of the child, but the parent's knowledge of the child's experience in nursery – real knowledge, not just an

Georgia (31 months) and Marilyn

Marilyn picks up Georgia when she comes to her and holds her lovingly and they watch the other children together. Georgia seems calmer and snuggles into her and watches the other children over the side of the wall sleepily. She seems to be more relaxed … Marilyn saunters back to the main body of the garden … Georgia is floppy and relaxed and Marilyn is holding her and stroking her affectionately. Georgia seems happy just to lie against her body now, even though Marilyn is talking to other adults

Georgia, who is often tense and restless at nursery, is able to relax and be still with her special person, Marilyn. Marilyn accepts her attachment, knowing its value for Georgia.

Jo

'The children need to be able to see your face and to know that you're there as they fall asleep.'

Jo has simply observed that if children know their key person is by their side, they feel secure enough to fall asleep

account of nappies changed and food eaten. It can offer parents peace of mind and a feeling of inclusion, making it possible to leave their child confidently and smoothly, especially if they can develop reassuring 'coming and going' routines with their child's key person.

There are benefits for the key person, too, including being aware of how much they matter to a child and her family, and of the impact they can have on her well-being and development. It may lead to greater job satisfaction and, in turn, lower staff turnover.

However, there are a number of barriers to using a key person approach. Some are organisational, for instance, pressures on staff and staffing and the unpredictability of staff absences. Many staff value the teamwork aspect of their work and may feel the key person system would undermine it. Equally, both parents and staff often say they value the opportunity given by nursery for children to mix with a wide variety of people and might not welcome the key person approach for that reason. In practice, there is no reason why a key person approach should prevent teamwork – getting to know individual children really well can facilitate teamwork when the knowledge is shared.

There may also be other misgivings. Some staff may worry about undermining a child's primary attachment relationship with their parents; others may find the intensity and intimacy of attachment difficult to handle. Staff need support to ponder the difference between affection and love, for instance. As a team, they may wish to consider what is meant by love in this context, and whether it is an appropriate feeling to incorporate into their professional relationships with children.

These are legitimate concerns but they need to be set against young children's very real need for personal, warm and consistent attention from a very few adults, who know them well.

KEYPOINTS

● Babies and young children need attachment relationships with the people who look after them in their daily lives.

● The key person approach can be used to help attachment relationships develop in the daycare situation.

● Children's key persons can be the cornerstone of a partnership between nursery and home, and help teamwork in the nursery.

Emmanuel (15 months) with Lucinda

Lucinda returns and Emmanuel wakes and is picked up by Lucinda – she asks him gently, 'Why do you look so serious?'. He nestles against her, looks relaxed and just as if he is struggling to regain his bearings. ... 'Right, are you allright now?' She sits on the floor pointing out a bus, but Emmanuel cries immediately. 'Oh, you're not ready to be put down?' and she puts him back on her lap.

Children may express their attachment to their key person by not wanting to be put down. Lucinda accepts that and gives him longer to 'come round' after his sleep. Although he is only 15 months old, Lucinda talks to him as if he could fully understand what she says, knowing that he will understand her tone of voice and her body language.

Lucinda about her relationship with Emmanuel

' ... because it's my first job, I've never experienced what it's like, there's such a lot of feelings. How can you tell ... there's a closeness and there isn't. Your key child wants you so you've got to be there for them but you have to balance it.'

2.3 Adults respond positively to children's expressions of attachment to their key persons

When adults respond to all the behaviours which come with attachment positively, with consistency and commitment, children experience the feeling of being loved and looked after, which enables them to grow, explore, reciprocate and learn.

Young children's attachment behaviours include making sure key adults remain nearby, crying for them if they move away, smiling and verbalising at them when close at hand, moving towards them when anxious. When this behaviour is directed at their key persons above all others, it shows there is real attachment.

Attachment is like a thread. Some days the thread is longer and more elastic than others! Some days the thread is short and brittle and the hard-pressed practitioner may need to allow the child to be physically close all day long.

The howls of protest when the key person tries to leave are just as much an indication of attachment as the more rewarding smiles and hugs. A child may also protest when her key person returns, as an expression of anger at being left in the first place.

For very young children, being physically held and caressed is part of the process and expression of attachment. This is an area of practice that requires great sensitivity. An attachment relationship is one of intimacy, involving all the senses. As a team, nursery staff need to have thought very carefully through the issues of child protection which protect both the

As Lucinda says, attachment relationships are a balancing act, but it is a balancing act worth managing.

Eileen

'Sometimes I do say, "Oh – my babies!" and the manager says "Oh – they're not your babies!" and I have to catch myself and say "Yes ... " but you do get emotionally involved ... they do get attached to you ... I don't know whether this is going to sound unprofessional, it's almost like being another mother ... things a mother would do like cuddles and making them feel secure – it's love – it's not what you learn in college, but it is love.'

Eileen is positive about the attachment relationships which develop, but aware of their complexity. She seems to feel a bit ambivalent about her position as 'almost like another mother'. These are important issues and it helps when staff can talk them through with each other and with their manager, and they are comfortable working within nursery guidelines and policies.

children and themselves. Nursery staff need to work within the agreed nursery policy. Key policies like this need to be revisited often.

As well as being held physically, being held in mind is also very important for young children. It helps them to negotiate the ups and down of the nursery day if they know that their special person is thinking of them, even if they cannot be with them all the time. While busy doing something else, the key person can keep contact with the child, maintaining the precious thread of attachment. This helps the child learn to trust that their Very Important Person will return.

An attachment relationship with an adult is the most helpful context for children to begin to learn how to manage and express their feelings. It also offers a powerful context for the positive power of modelling behaviour and attitudes. Some carers' responses to children's attachment may be complicated by worry about managing their own feelings in relation to a child, including fearing feelings of loss when a child whom they have come to love moves on. Such fears can lead to a desire to protect oneself by not making the commitment that is a necessary part of attachment. This applies to professional relationships as much as to personal ones.

Although potentially very rewarding, the key person approach is certainly intense, hard work and a big commitment. The relationship makes heavy demands upon the key person, which need to be understood, planned for and supported by the nursery policies and management.

KEYPOINTS

- It helps when adults respond positively to children's expressions of attachment.
- For children, being held in mind can be as important as being held physically.
- The key person approach is a big commitment but can be very rewarding for both children and adults.

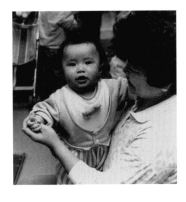

Conclusion

Affection and attachment are vital for young children's well-being. Attachment relationships are particularly important and require special sensitivity and skill from practitioners. Practitioners may have a number of concerns about the key person system and attachment in general.

Some practitioners may be anxious about assuming a parental role or even of taking some of the love properly due to the parent. It is safe to say that even very young babies will not confuse their carer with their parent and they are more likely to suffer from the lack of a close personal relationship at nursery. If practitioners are able to establish close professional relationships with both children and their parents, the two different experiences of attachment for the child can be complementary and greatly enhance the quality of her experience of being in daycare.

QUESTIONS FOR REFLECTION

- What are your feelings about attachment between children and staff? Is it right for staff to have 'special' children or should they treat all children the same?
- Do you think a key person approach is a good idea? What are the possible drawbacks?
- Do you worry about taking on a parental role or is this something to aspire to?
- In your nursery, is enough time and space given to transition times – the dropping off and collecting times? Are parents encouraged to stay a while and develop a reassuring 'comings and goings' routine for their child?

3. Physical care

Children's physical care is generally given high priority in daycare settings. Staff are vigilant about safety, nappy changes are carried out frequently and children rarely have to wait for food or drink. Sleeping babies are checked on at regular intervals.

Most of the staff interviewed in the study aspired to achieving personal and individual care. However, in practice, physical care is often shared between all staff members for at least some of the day. After all, making sure all the children are fed, clean and rested is a physically demanding task and a heavy responsibility. In many nurseries, this responsibility is met by careful teamwork: monitoring of sleeping children by all staff, rotas of nappy changing and meal times and the ritual of group nap times. This can make it hard to achieve personal care. Given the desire for sharing tasks and the other pressures of the day, physical care can easily becoming depersonalised and the individual pace, rhythm and preferences of each child can get lost.

The youngest children in particular need to experience personal care and, if we observe them, they show us that they mind when an adult who has not become close and familiar undertakes intimate tasks. Even two-year-olds who have come to enjoy the sociability of shared meal times and sleep times will sometimes need more personalised, one-to-one care.

Debbie

'So for me, when I change a nappy, I'm not doing it as a routine, it's a chance to have a special time. ... It's important to make the most of that special time and to build up the relationship ... The danger with 15 children being changed three or four times a day is that it can become routine – more routine than we would like.'
Debbie is keen to avoid the 'conveyor belt' feeling about

3.1 One or two key persons only carry out the tasks of feeding, dressing, helping children use the lavatory, giving medicine and settling them to sleep

Children's physical care is inseparable from their emotional care. Particularly for babies and the youngest children, feeding and changing are episodes of great intimacy. If these kinds of tasks are shared between a staff team, a three-month-old baby can in the course of one day find herself being fed and changed by five or six different adults. The difficulty is that neither babies *physical care and sees it as a valuable and enjoyable opportunity for getting to know each other.*

Evie (16 months) with Marilyn

08.43 Once again, Evie returns to the fruit and vegetables by the shop. Now Marilyn says, 'Right, Evie – can I change your nappy – Evie, can I change your nappy, please? Evie, are you ignoring me? Oh, look, and you're playing so nicely – put them back in – good girl – come and do your nappy.'
08.44 Marilyn waits as Evie puts the food items back into the shopping basket one by one and lifts the basket to carry it with her.
08.45 'Right, come and do your nappy, Evie – we can come straight back, I promise.'
08.46 Marilyn lays Evie down gently on the changing mat. Evie holds a little toy … All the while Evie is fingering the small toy, turning it, looking at it and then she drops it. 'Oh dear – you've dropped it.'
08.49 'Are you going back to play in the shop?'
Marilyn asks Evie if she can interrupt her play in order to change her nappy, and then waits for her, rather than just sweeping her away from what she is doing. Marilyn then helps Evie keep in mind what she was doing before the nappy change interrupted her flow. She handles and speaks to Evie gently.

nor adults have the capacity to establish so many relationships of intimacy.

Very young children *do* mind who manages their intimate care needs and they sometimes show signs of unhappiness and stress when their favourite adults are not available. They may seek their attention and comfort by crying, rocking or pulling at their own hair or clothes, sucking objects, or by retreating to a favourite refuge such as a bean bag or beneath a table.

If physical care is carried out by the one or two key persons to whom a child has become attached, knows and trusts, then care tasks can be personalised to take account of the child as an individual with an individual's preferences.

Routines will more quickly become familiar and enjoyable for a baby if she does not have to get used to many different people's ways of handling her. Even if there is a common routine, each individual staff member will inevitably do things a bit differently, which can be unsettling for a baby.

There are many ways of making physical care a personal interaction rather than a 'conveyor belt'. Adults can address the child by name and make sustained eye or verbal contact. During a nappy change, for example, the child can be offered a particular object to hold and the carer can chat to the child about what is going on, or what the child was doing when she had to be interrupted. This helps the child pick up the thread of her play afterwards, and shows that she is being treated as a whole person and not just a little body that needs cleaning up! The care routine becomes more consistent and the child feels more secure and 'held'.

As children grow, they become capable of feeding themselves and better able to express their own preferences; they may start to enjoy the sociability of shared meal times and sleep times. They often show their enjoyment of group routines and the sense of security they can bring. However, there will still be times when they will need more individualised care one-to-one from their own special person.

KEYPOINTS

- Very young children do mind who manages their intimate care needs.
- Care tasks can be personalised to take account of a child's individual preferences.
- Physical care can become a valuable and enjoyable time to get to know each other.

Jan about Andrew (7 months)

'Getting him to sleep, well, it depends on his mood. He likes the blanket close to his face, and his musical clown from home, and he usually goes off to sleep alone, but other times when he is a bit upset he likes to be cuddled in. ... When he is being fed with a spoon you have to do it as quickly as possible, and not have many gaps between spoon feeds or he doesn't like it, and he prefers puddings. He likes to be cuddled in when he has a bottle, and he usually closes his eyes.'

Jan, as Andrew's key person, has got to know him very much as an individual, with individual preferences. Using this knowledge supports Andrew's well-being and makes her the 'expert' about him. She can share her knowledge of him with other members of the team.

Rachel

'Normally, we are supposed to change a child as soon as they wake from their sleep, but I know with Rosie that she hates

3.2 Physical care for the youngest children is personalised, being based on not only the child's physical needs, but also on sensitive observation of the child's emotional state and knowledge of her preferred routines

When physical care is personalised, it reaches another level of quality: it is more likely to meet that particular child's needs on that particular day; it offers an opportunity for high-quality personal interaction, deepening relationships between children and adults; it also offers valuable opportunities for children's learning. (See A3.3, *Physical care* on p.28.)

The problem in many daycare settings is that, although individual staff members are sensitive to children's preferences and mood, the way the work is organised makes it difficult for them to be flexible. The nursery as an institution has other priorities and pressures. Sleeps, feeds and nappy changes happen because it is the time of day for them to happen, rather than as a response to an individual child's hunger, tiredness or the state of their nappies. Staff feel under pressure of time to get everything done. When staff are feeling under pressure, the children are too!

If carers are free to be flexible, they can use their powers of observation and empathy to adjust care routines to the needs of the child. Even the youngest baby will have developed distinctive preferences by the to be undressed and changed when she has just been asleep and all warm and, if I insist, she grizzles and won't settle to anything afterwards. So I asked Julie (the supervisor) about it, and she said it would be OK to wait. I also checked with Rosie's mum and she said she was just the same at home and not to worry – there are worse things than a wet nappy.'

Rachel, a junior member of staff, became aware of a difference between the nursery expectation that babies are changed immediately after a sleep and Rosie's individual response, which would put her 'out of sorts' for a while after the unwanted nappy change. She checked it out with her supervisor and with Rosie's mum, and they were able to share their knowledge of her. Rachel was then able to adjust the nursery routine to suit her as an individual person.

time she starts in nursery. By finding out about them from parents and adjusting nursery routines accordingly, it is possible to create some comforting echoes of home at nursery. Conversely, some parents are keen to adopt some nursery routines at home – especially when they have been impressed to see their two-year-old enjoy sitting down to eat, for instance. All this creates more continuity and security for the child.

Using the key person approach, a child's special adult will get to know her well enough to know her general preferences. She will also be able to observe her behaviour that day and judge her emotional state. She will be able to judge when she is, for example, unsettled and worried about something and therefore needs a longer settling to sleep routine than normal. What is more, she can share her knowledge of her preferences and her mood with any other staff who may need to care for her. She becomes the expert on that child, just as at home her parents are the experts.

KEYPOINTS

- When physical care is personalised, it reaches another level of quality.
- If carers are free to be flexible, they can adjust care routines to the needs of the child.
- A key person gets to know a child's preferences and can read her moods; she can also share that knowledge with others.

Gloria

'Well, when I first came, I didn't know about nappies – I'd never worked in a day nursery, but now it is one of my favourite parts of the job! We sing to them, and we have some animal pictures up by where we change the nappies, so we are learning about those. David picks up his nappy from the basket and he likes making the animal noises while I'm changing his nappy.'

3.3 Physical care is used as an opportunity for informal learning

Meeting children's personal care needs can be seen as an endless round of chores and the best a carer can do is to get them over with quickly so the child can go back to her play. It may seem overwhelmingly difficult to give each child consistent and personalised physical care, such as they might receive at home. On the other hand, feeding a baby, dressing a wriggly one-year-old or taking a two-year-old to the lavatory can be opportunities not only for affection and getting to know one another, but also for informal, everyday learning.

Georgia (31 months) with Marilyn

Marilyn affectionately changes her nappy and fixes it on as she lies on the changing mat. Georgia has her bottom washed, it is unhurried and they play 'round and round the garden' together. Georgia is laughing and seems to enjoy the physical intimate play and this special humorous and close interaction that she is having with Marilyn. Marilyn unhurriedly sings with her about what she is doing. She makes up a song about the size of the nappy, about it being too small. When it is finally finished she playfully jumps her off with a big jumping movement and then bumps her down rather abruptly because she notices that Viktor in playing with wee in his potty …

During this changing episode, Marilyn is unhurried, humorous and inventive. She gives the impression that they are both enjoying the time together. The episode actually ends with a bump, as Marilyn's attention has to be given to a minor emergency, which is typical of the multiple demands made on staff in a busy nursery.

Babies and children are learning all the time and they learn from everything that happens during their day, not just the bits which adults might see as a learning activity, such as doing a puzzle or playing with letters. Conversation and give-and-take games during physical care can help children's language development. Young children need to hear lots of language before they are ready to speak in words. A simple running commentary on what is happening provides a warm bath of words for the child. They will also understand from the carer's tone of voice that all this inconvenient fussing, for example, getting dressed, is OK and quite bearable. In fact, it can become a pleasure!

Songs and rhymes can help turn the chore into a shared pleasure and again these will help a child's language to develop. A child's key person will know the child's favourite rhymes and they can become a valued part of the routine. The key person will also know something of the child's interests, which can be woven in too. Again, the carer will know which are the child's favourite stories at the moment and be able to weave them into the conversation.

With slightly older children, there are opportunities for talking about subjects of interest to them. Lavatories, for instance, are subjects of great interest to many two-year-olds! Where does the water (let alone anything else) go after all that flushing?

As children get older, they can be encouraged to play an active part in care routines by, for instance, fetching their blanket before a sleep or choosing and holding the nappy during a change. This helps them feel involved and competent, which helps their self-esteem grow.

KEYPOINTS

- Physical care is a rich opportunity for everyday learning.
- Chat, songs and rhymes really help their development.
- When children play an active part in daily routines, it helps them feel good about themselves.

Conclusion

Young children *do* mind who meets their intimate care needs and they will benefit from being cared for by one or two adults they have come to know and trust and who can personalise care routines to their needs and preferences. Physical care then becomes a valuable one-to-one opportunity for enriching relationships and for enjoying informal learning.

Children with lots of individualised loving care and special routines at home may be readier to enjoy group routines at nursery. Conversely, children without this experience in their home lives may need more individualised care for longer. In a setting which uses a key person approach, staff are more likely to be able to pick up on these individual differences and respond to them flexibly.

QUESTIONS FOR REFLECTION

- Why do babies and young children need personalised physical care?
- How can staff get to know a child's preferences?
- How could physical care be organised to meet children's individual needs?
- How can staff make the most of getting children dressed, or of meal times?

4. Setting limits

Most of us hate situations in which we have no control, no 'say'. It feels stressful and difficult. On the other hand, we also like to know 'where we stand' in a given situation and what the rules of behaviour are. In a similar way, nursery rules and routines can be experienced both as a source of security and satisfaction for young children and as a very unwelcome tyranny. As one- and two-year-olds are only rarely given a 'say' in what they do, eat, wear, etc, they are particularly sensitive about being told what to do – hence the outright rebellions and tantrums which can make life with toddlers so difficult.

It helps if adults say *yes* as much as they can, but when they say *no*, they mean it. Limits which are inconsistently applied are confusing and undermining – a child never knows 'where she stands'. On the other hand, limits and rules which are too rigid do not allow for children's expressions of individuality as they develop as people. It is all a balancing act. Limits, rules and routines require a lot of staff thought, and it helps children to accept them when adults explain them clearly but gently, in a way they can understand.

Rachel
We try not to have too many rules, but those we do have, we stick to – mostly those are to do with safety, although really for children this age, it is mostly a case of making sure the environment is safe, rather than telling them not to touch something. We used to insist that all the children have a sleep after lunch, but then there were one or two who'd had a sleep in the morning already or who, for one reason or another, just couldn't settle. So now most children do have a sleep, but we just have it as a quiet time for the others. If I'm not doing things in

4.1 The limits set by adults are kept to the minimum, are consistent, and support the children's security and well-being

If limits set are kept to the minimum, and adults say yes to children as often as they can, children will feel better about themselves and the things they want to do. Quite a few limits are for reasons of safety. Most carers are acutely aware of safety risks, and work conscientiously within their nursery's health and safety guidelines, but concerns for safety need to be balanced against the young child's need to explore and take safe risks, that is, minor risks within a safe environment. After all, a one-year-old could be kept physically very safe in a play pen all day, but what would she learn and how would she feel about herself?

the kitchen, I like to have that time for a quiet one-to-one story with someone.'

Marilyn
'If they have done something naughty, 'naughty' is a word we don't use. We point out the hurt of their actions ... Our real concern is not just with the two-year-old now, but for the long term person they are going to become.'
In 'pointing out the hurt of their actions' Marilyn is suggesting that they are helping children understand the consequences of their actions for other people. She is aware of how important it is that children's behaviour is managed skilfully and positively in the earliest years.

Aisha's mother
'They tidy up early so they can go home on time so the children have nothing to play with ... And going to sleep – they may not be tired, but they still have to go to sleep. So it's a case of one on the potty, all on the potty. One go to sleep, all go to sleep. You can point it out to the key worker, but they still do it.
This is an example of a nursery organised to suit its own organisational needs, not those of the children. Aisha's mother is clearly not happy about it, because she can see that Aisha can't be thought of and treated as an individual in a set-up like this.

If limits and rules are kept to a minimum, they are also more likely to be enforceable, as children are more likely to accept a small number, and adults do not get too worn out, struggling to enforce too many. Having too many rules can give children the feeling that they are incompetent and can have no 'say'. In these circumstances, one can land up with compliant but resentful children or children who have switched off and just wait for the next adult instruction.

It is also important to be consistent, as inconsistency is confusing and undermining for children. What are they to think if one day it is fine to run out into the garden in your socks, funny even, and the next it is treated as very naughty? Moreover, if a two-year-old is feeling rebellious, how can she manage to rebel effectively if she is not clear what the limit is that day? She will still feel rebellious, but have nowhere to put it! Timid children may give up trying anything on at all and more reckless children may try everything just to see what happens.

Limits and routines are needed which support children's well-being and security. Staff are often hard-pressed, but it is important to think together and to keep checking, 'Why do we do this?' Sometimes rules develop because of pressures on staff and on time. All institutions develop their ways of doing things, but they need to be kept under review. It helps when staff keep returning to what the purpose of a rule is and checking that it is for the benefit of the children.

KEYPOINTS

- It helps when nursery rules are kept to the minimum, but are consistent.
- Children need rules and routines that support their well-being.
- It helps when staff keep checking with each other, 'Why do we do this?'

Georgia (31 months) and Marilyn

Georgia is agitated, but in an excitably happy way this time. Georgia goes over to the dressing-up rail and pulls off a garment. Marilyn says, 'We can't play with them if you pull them and put them on the floor'. Marilyn encourages her to pick the things off the floor and then says strongly, 'Good girl, Georgia', while she insistently models how to pick things off the floor. ... Marilyn has guided her hand insistently and made her pick the clothes up off the floor, at the same time giving her the positive feedback.

Georgia is having a difficult day and Marilyn, with whom she has a close relationship, supports her to accept a limit on her behaviour, explaining why clothes shouldn't be pulled off the rails onto the floor, modelling how to put it right and giving positive feedback. She is firm and warm with her. Some people might think that just modelling picking up the clothes was enough, rather than guiding Georgia's hand as well.

4.2 When adults set limits on children's behaviour, they explain them clearly but sympathetically

It helps children accept limits on their behaviour when adults explain them clearly but sympathetically. It is inevitable that setting limits will cause feelings of frustration, as adults are stopping children doing what they want to do. Instead of just saying *no*, it helps to sympathise, and explain carefully why the limit is necessary. Even though many of the children won't understand all of what is said, they will understand the tone and the body language.

There is a big difference to a child between a limit applied harshly, in a way which appears to deny her needs ('I don't care if you are hungry now, we don't have our snack until three o'clock'), and a limit applied consistently, but more sympathetically ('Poor you! Are you hungry already? Do you think you can hang on until three o'clock which is when we have our snack? You can? Fantastic!') The second approach is more likely to work in terms of managing behaviour and stands a chance of improving her self-esteem rather than damaging it. This is because her feelings and needs are accepted, even if they can't be met straight away. Being sympathetic about a child's frustration with a limit does not mean that she is allowed to break it.

Even with careful explanation of limits and rules, children under three have a lot more living to do before they can fully appreciate why they are necessary. It takes a great deal of experience to learn about consequences of actions and appreciate other people's needs. However, if young children see a rule applied fairly to everyone, they will begin to see its advantages – after all, if each person can have only one biscuit, it stops someone else eating the lot!

It will be clear that sympathising and explaining about limits has been worth it not only when they are increasingly easily accepted, but also when nursery rules are played out in the imaginative play area. Children 'work through' new ideas and experiences in their imaginative play. Two-year-olds can take out their feelings about being controlled by imposing rules on the dolls – they may well be a more draconian version of nursery rules. They may also enjoy carefully settling the dolls to sleep just as they themselves are settled, with a reassuringly consistent sequence of events, which reminds them that they are loved and looked after.

KEYPOINTS

● It helps children to accept limits on their behaviour when adults explain them clearly but sympathetically.
● Being sympathetic about a child's frustration with a rule does not mean that she is allowed to break it.

David (21 months)
'David is fast asleep in a buggy with his own blanket (his comfort object) and his dummy; six other children are also asleep in various places, including a double buggy, while most of the cots stand empty; the children who are not asleep are playing at putting dolls to sleep … The staff member with them encourages them to be very quiet and joins in the play, rocking and patting the 'babies', supporting the children's imaginative game.
In David's nursery there is an expectation and a routine that all children will have a rest at this time of day, but the routine allows for a wide range of individual variation – David clearly prefers his buggy and his own blanket from home, other children have chosen their favourite places and the staff member helps the remaining children, who are not ready to sleep, to play gentle games putting dolls to sleep.

4.3 The limits set allow for children's expressions of individuality and home routines and customs

Without limits, rules and routines group care for children from birth to three would be very difficult, if not impossible. However, it is important to remember that babies and children are individual people, with individual preferences, moods and individual families, home routines and customs. As it is an important part of children's well-being that they are recognised as individuals, the limits set need to allow for some flexibility.

Most daycare staff are aware of the value of knowing about children's home routines and customs, and the parents' attitude to setting limits. This can be an area for real exchange and learning (see C2, *Staff–parent relationships* on p.67). It can be very helpful to find out about any special going to sleep routines and rituals which a child has developed at home. After all, how many adults sleep well on the first night of a stay away from home? Similarly, while perhaps the majority of under-threes show little desire for privacy during changing or toilet times, some children and families may feel it is important.

One way of allowing for children's individuality is to give them choices. In practice, these need to be genuine but

Sam (11 months)

The staff member was observed settling Sam in his cot, with a toy in his hand, knowing that he will turn himself full circle in the cot before he settles to sleep.

Sam's carer has got to know his preferred way of settling himself to sleep. She is unlikely to insist that his head goes at the 'proper' end of the cot! She will also know that she can safely leave him once he is settled like this.

limited. It is possible to give young children real choices and respect their decisions. This gives them a sense of control and self-respect, and encourages their active participation. Nursery staff can feel the pressure of parental expectation, for instance, about how a child is dressed. However, if they explain that David (21 months) has one blue sock and one pink-and-white-stripy one *because he chose them himself* and it is important for him to have his choices respected where it is possible, then most parents will understand.

Part of children's individuality lies in their interests and their favourite play patterns or schemas* (see D1.2 in *Supporting children's interests* on p.78). If parents can shed some light on what their interests are at home, and this knowledge is put together with what is observed in nursery, it may be possible to build them into the child's nursery routines. It may also help in sensitively but firmly applying limits on behaviour. Allowing for children's individual home routines and customs is not always easy. A staff member in the study commented, for instance:

> 'Sometimes … parents ask us not to take their baby into the garden because they are afraid they will get too cold – we have to respect their ideas – we cannot say we have another opinion.'

If parent–staff relationships of mutual respect can be established, it may be possible to discuss issues like this more fully.

KEYPOINTS

- Young children are individuals.
- Nursery limits, rules and routines need to allow for some individual flexibility.
- It helps to find out about home routines and parental attitudes.

Conclusion

In setting limits for the children, it helps when adults carefully explain them, and the reason for them, showing their sympathy for the frustration that limits and rules can cause. It helps children accept limits when adults make sure they are consistently applied and kept to the minimum.

Part of the balancing act is being consistent, but also being flexible enough to allow for children's expressions of individual difference and their home routines and customs. To make sure that limits and rules are ultimately for the children's benefit, staff need to keep going back to their purpose.

QUESTIONS FOR REFLECTION

- Which rules are necessary, which are flexible and which are negotiable?
- How do staff respond when a child does not accept a limit?
- How can possible causes of frustration and conflict for children be minimised?
- Does it matter if home rules and routines are completely different from nursery ones? If so, should the nursery adjust its rules to suit the family or should parents adopt nursery ways?

5. Valuing and respecting differences between people

It helps children to value themselves and others when they are supported by adults who treat everyone with equal respect, and with equal concern, and who positively value the things which make them distinctive such as their ethnicity, home languages, religion, culture, family structure or any disability.

Children build up a picture very gradually about the differences between people. Through becoming aware of differences, children can gain an understanding of similarities. Attitudes and practices in the daycare setting can help them learn that the culture of their own family is valued and respected alongside others.

In settings where both children and staff share a similar cultural background, it is important that staff introduce, discuss and reflect differences between people in positive ways on a regular basis and build it into their planning. As children and adults alike can feel apprehensive about differences, or even threatened, it is important that staff offer a warmly positive approach. When adults recognise and challenge bias, stereotypes and discriminatory attitudes and behaviour in a positive and sensitive way, then children are likely to learn to do the same.

Rachel

'We think it's important to welcome all the children in the morning with their name, you know, saying 'Hello, Tamara, hello, Finn' – and hello to the parents and carers too. It's a lot of names to remember, but we think it's worth it. After all, how that handing-over time goes can affect the whole day. We also do the 'Hello' song at circle time – the children love it.'

In this nursery, the staff know how important it is to give a warm and individual greeting to

5.1 There is a warm welcome for everyone entering the setting; adults actively emphasise and positively value differences between people

A universal welcome is a powerful thing. Most nursery staff know how important it is to give a warm, individual greeting to each child as she arrives and to be welcoming to her parents. This welcome also applies just as much to a temporary member of staff starting her shift, the person delivering the day's milk or the engineer who has come to fix the boiler.

From the child's point of view, all this shows that

each child, and to the parents or carers who bring them. Children's names, and the ways in which they are used, are a very important part of their developing self-concept and, clearly, the nursery's 'Hello' song has become a favourite. Recognising everyone as an individual helps young children to begin to understand what it is to be part of a group.

Sam (11 months) and Aziza

Now Aziza has arrived. She seems to be immediately involved with the children, greeting and touching them as she enters the nursery … Aziza picks Sam up now … she carries him to a large play mat … sitting him gently down on it. She sits down with him, inviting other children to sit with them.

Aziza makes all the children feel welcome, greeting them with her voice and by touch. She settles with her key child, Sam, and makes sure she includes an invitation to other children to join her on the mat.

everyone is welcome and everyone is valued. She sees that there are not some people or some groups of people who are more welcome than others; everyone is welcomed and treated with respect. In an environment like this, a young child can have confidence that her family background is viewed positively. She can develop positive judgements about both genders, about disability, about ethnic, cultural, linguistic or religious groups, her own and those of other people.

Young children are curious and observant. They will notice and be interested in differences. Why does another child's hair look and feel so different from her own? Why does one child have a special shoe? Why does a third need injections? Some children live in families which feel threatened by differences between people and express that feeling by being openly or covertly hostile to people they perceive as different. Their attitudes and behaviour may convey to their children that some people are 'not like us', and therefore inferior. It is important that the setting offers a warmly positive approach to differences.

Sometimes people say, 'We treat them all the same'. This is not as helpful as it sounds. It can mean that staff and children are discouraged from noticing and commenting on difference and children may receive awkward reactions when they do. It may also indicate that, although staff wish to treat all children equally, in fact, they treat all children as if they were white and able-bodied. Judgemental comments or negative reactions to difference from children are firmly addressed, but children may be left confused or may just draw the conclusion that it is all right to feel like that (that is, hostile), but not to express their feelings. They may even get the message that the difference itself is 'not nice'. Children can feel uncomfortable when confronted by differences because this is a reaction which often accompanies something which doesn't fit in with prior experience. It really helps when adults can offer a safe place for children to express this discomfort and talk together about differences in an open, positive and sensitive way.

Tess

'We had the theme of 'Myself'. We talked about who lives in their house with them and we tell them that all the families are different and we talk about the different brothers and sisters. Different families do different things.'

Children are curious and often interested in differences, and it helps when adults talk to them about differences in positive and non-judgemental ways. Some nurseries like to plan around themes, but what matters most is everyday and ongoing conversation and attitudes.

A genuinely helpful approach is to welcome everyone and treat them as individuals, not making any assumptions about their cultural background, but getting to know them as people. While general knowledge about a range of cultural traditions can be useful background, there are wide individual variations within families. Where staff are unsure, for instance, about a child's dietary needs, the simplest and most helpful thing to do is to ask her parents.

Many daycare settings seek to value diversity by celebrating festivals from a variety of traditions, often with a craft activity. When thinking about which festivals to celebrate and how to celebrate them, particularly with such young children, it is worth pausing to think about what children who are under three might learn from the celebration. If they are helping to get ready for the celebration by making decorations, for instance, or by making a card, the most important question is, 'What will the children be learning about the people whose culture this festival belongs to?'

When, as we know, cultures and languages are already ranked in a hierarchy of value and importance, just celebrating a festival will do little to alter the messages a child receives from society. It is important to address the differences between people's lives every day of the year, not just on special occasions.

Good early years practice is planned around the needs and interests of individual children. In order to convey positive messages about differences between people, this will also need to include a sound knowledge of children's backgrounds and to take account of the disadvantages and discrimination which certain groups in society experience (see D3.2 in *Providing a learning environment* on p.90).

KEYPOINTS

- Children are curious and often interested in differences.
- It helps to talk to them about differences in positive and non-judgemental ways.
- It helps children to value themselves and others when everyone is made welcome and treated as an individual.

Michèle

'I am keen to learn about children's cultures – I always encourage staff to be open. For example, Sarah was vegetarian because (her mother) did not want to say she needed Kosher food. I love to hear different languages – it's got to be an asset to them later.'

Michèle has learned that parents don't always find it easy to tell nursery staff about their cultural background and needs. It is not just a question of encouraging staff to be open, but building up relationships of trust and acceptance with parents, so that they can be sure that they, and their culture, will be valued and made welcome.

Vikram's father

'I'm a foreigner myself from Bangladesh so I speak Bengali. When I first came, we decided to speak English all the time but the teacher came and said, 'No, that's not good, they can learn both languages – it is good for them'. My English is not very good and so I might be teaching them wrong at home, so we speak Bengali at home and they learn English at nursery …

They are always celebrating different festivals here as well – for us we are going to be celebrating 'Durga puja'. We have a celebration in the nursery too and we celebrate at home and meet up with family in the East End of London – It goes on for four or five days.

The staff in Vikram's nursery have encouraged his father to value their home language, as well as the English Vikram is learning in the English-speaking

5.2 Staff form positive relationships with parents and take account of differences between families

Rather than treating all the children 'the same', it is more helpful to respond to children as individuals. This entire framework is based on the assumption that children's well-being is enhanced when their experiences in the two settings of home and daycare are complementary rather than contradictory.

When the home routines and cultural practices with which the children are most familiar are, as far as practicable, carried over into their daycare setting, children are likely to experience a far greater sense of security and belonging than when there is a break in continuity or only minimal overlap between home and nursery.

The efforts which staff make to consult and involve parents are very important. Some parents are very keen for their child, even very young babies, to adapt quickly to nursery patterns. They take pride in how quickly and completely they fit in. However, most will appreciate a nursery's willingness to take account of their culture, home languages, religion and ethnicity.

It is still important not to make assumptions. Knowing a child or family's ethnic background can lead to false assumptions about their religious observance. It can also lead to false assumptions about culture. For example, just because a child is of African-Caribbean appearance does not mean that she will particularly enjoy reggae music. She might, but so might a white child. In this, as in other aspects of culture, it helps when all the children are offered the opportunity of experiencing and enjoying a wide range.

The best way for staff to learn about a child's family background is by talking to her parents – and to keep on talking to them. Similarly, talking with staff is the only way that parents can know enough about a setting's practice to feel secure about the continuity between home and daycare, or confident enough to raise any troubling issues. Also, if parents know that *nursery environment. It is enormously helpful when parents and staff can talk to each other about these issues. Vikram's father also seems to find the celebration of festivals at home and in the daycare setting complementary. From the staff's point of view, Vikram's father could make a very valuable contribution – lots of the slightly older children would be very interested in hearing about a celebration which goes on for four or five days!*

Sam's mother

'We speak Hebrew at home. So the nursery have asked for a list of words so that they can know if Sam uses any of them..'
Sam's carers are keen to recognise his first words and to value his home culture.

their family's culture or skin colour or a child's disability are acknowledged and welcomed, they are more likely to be willing to contribute and this will provide a valuable resource for the nursery.

In taking account of children's home background, staff need practical strategies for responding adequately to children's home language(s). While many white English adults see their monolingualism as the norm, in the world as a whole, it is the exception.

It is important to recognise and value the bilingualism of many young children and to confirm with parents that *both* languages matter, especially the home one. The experience of learning one language is very valuable for learning a second – or a third!

Staff can help a child learning a second or third language by having confidence that the child will learn it through listening, talking and doing things together (just as she learned her home language) and by remembering that understanding spoken language comes before using it. It helps enormously if staff in daycare settings are aware of the importance of non-verbal communication and respond to eye contact, gesture and body language.

KEYPOINTS

- Children feel more secure when the approaches of home and daycare are complementary.
- It is important not to make assumptions about children's family background.
- It helps when staff and parents can talk to each other and work in partnership, especially when staff learn a few friendly words of a home language.
- Children learn a second or third language just as they learn their first: through listening, talking and doing things together.

Georgia (31 months) and Richard

10.15 Georgia is sitting on the carpet with Kath and Richard (a child with hemiplegia and epilepsy). Richard is having some special exercises for his legs which are in splints. Georgia is very interested in Richard's physiotherapy and is familiar with the exercises. ... She wants to help and offers a bandage and splints to Kath ...

10.20 Georgia holds the book of physiotherapy instructions for Kath. Kath involves Georgia in the work with the bandage. Georgia leafs through the book and watches Kath giving the exercises to Richard. She sits with her legs spread and holds the exercise instruction book, and 'reads' the pages. ...

Children learn their attitudes towards difference from their important adults. Here, Georgia is eagerly picking up Kath's modelling of care and respect for Richard, a child with special needs.

Rachel

It's lovely having a male worker now – that's Craig. You can see the boys looking to him. We like to be a bit proactive about this 'boys can't wear dresses' stuff in the home corner. Finn's older sister has just got married and the other day Craig was in there with a bridal veil on his head and all the children, girls and boys, were decked out in their finery for a wedding. They looked so fabulous that we took some photos to go up on the wall.

Children and practitioners in our predominantly female-staffed nurseries can greatly benefit from the presence and

5.3 Discriminatory and judgemental behaviour and prejudiced attitudes are clearly and sensitively challenged

In order to feel safe, children need to know that prejudiced attitudes and discriminatory and judgemental behaviour are unacceptable. In such young children, it will only rarely be possible to distinguish discriminatory behaviour from plain aggressive behaviour, but there may well be negative judgements about physical differences and disability and sometimes racial prejudice and racial discrimination can surface in two-year-olds.

These things can be handled in just the same way as other forms of unacceptable behaviour: consistently, sensitively and with the child's security and well-being in mind. It is especially important to explain why such behaviour is unacceptable. Much of this explaining can be conveyed through body language and tone of voice.

There may also be times when boys or girls seek to exclude the others from an activity, or they ridicule a child who steps over a perceived gender divide (for example, a boy dressing up as a bride or princess). When they are talking to toddlers, adults can help by not linking occupations to gender, as people do when they assume that doctors are men and nurses are women.

Adult expectations are important. Adults can expect and encourage exuberant and adventurous behaviour in both girls and boys, whilst also respecting the needs of all young children to be apart and observe at other times. Adult expectations of children with disabilities are equally significant and can limit or expand their potential.

It is important to challenge – equally clearly and sensitively – prejudiced attitudes or discriminatory and judgemental behaviour in the adults in the nursery, whether staff members, parents or visitors. Supposing a staff member introduces a new child as 'one of eight', and rolls her eyes upwards. She would be making a negative judgement about the size of the child's family, and this would need to be addressed. Although this can be done in a thought-provoking and non-humiliating *involvement of male staff. Adults are in a powerful position to model attitudes and values to children. Just being present in a particular area of the nursery shows that you value it.*

way, it is difficult, and managers need to realise that staff can feel threatened by even the most sensitive comment. For everyone's support, every setting needs to have clear policies and strategies in this area, which are the subject of ongoing debate and support within the staff team. This approach helps to ensure that the daycare setting is a place of universal welcome, where everyone feels safe.

KEYPOINTS

- Discriminatory behaviour should be sensitively but clearly challenged.
- Adult expectations, for instance about gender or disability, are important.

Conclusion

This is a challenging area of practice. It is clear from the study that there is currently some confusion amongst staff. Some choose not to think too deeply about it, and are therefore content with their nursery's practice, while others are aware of the challenges, but unclear what to do. It is important not to hide behind vague generalities, nor to be content with celebrating well-known festivals, but to think clearly through the differences which exist between the children and families who use early years services, to be observant and to continually gain new knowledge. The framework can offer a supportive starting point for moving towards a fuller understanding of good practice in this area.

Children need adult support to have appropriate respect for themselves and for others who are different from them, so that they can be confident and interact easily with others from a range of different backgrounds. All children, whether from a 'minority' or the 'majority' background, come from families with a culture and individual values and ideas to contribute to the setting. Gradually they develop an understanding of their own rights and those of others. They develop ideas about fairness and justice. Eventually, on the sound basis laid down in the early years, they will develop the self-confidence and understanding to stand up for themselves and others against biased ideas and discriminatory behaviour.

QUESTIONS FOR REFLECTION

- Does anything get in the way of offering everyone a warm welcome?
- Think about how you greet children on arrival. If you comment on the clothes they are wearing that day, what messages do your comments convey?
- How can nursery staff and parents work together to ensure the children's experiences in the two settings are both consistent and complementary?
- Are staff aware which countries 'Asian' parents come from and which languages are spoken at home?
- How can any language barriers between staff and parents be overcome?
- How can parents be helped to contribute to your setting?

B. RELATIONSHIPS: CHILD–CHILD

Introduction

This section is all about very young children's relationships with each other. It contains three elements. Number one is about how adults support children's relationship with themselves: their self-concept. Children who feel good about themselves, that is, have a positive self-concept, are much more likely to be able to relate well to others and to be happy and successful learners.

Element number two is about the ways in which adults value and encourage very young children's developing capacity for friendship with each other: recognising their strong interest in each other, encouraging their give-and-take games and offering children with similar interests the opportunity to play together.

Number three is about supporting children as they learn to participate in larger groups, and the variety of ways they communicate and behave in them, some of which can be hard for adults to handle! Children have a lot to learn about being in a group situation and adults can help them in many ways.

1. Self-concept

Children learn about themselves through their relationships with others. Their ideas about themselves are very much influenced by other people's ideas about them. It is from other people that they learn what they are good at and what they are bad at and whether they are lovable or unlovable, a misery or a ray of sunshine, clever or stupid, wanted or not wanted.

Children who feel good about themselves, that is, have a positive self-concept, are much more likely to be able to relate well to others and to be happy and successful learners. Their confidence in themselves grows when they know that other people – especially those they are close to – are noticing them, thinking about them, interested in them and wanting to be with them. Nurturing children's self-concept is as important as providing food and rest and keeping them clean.

As a person's sense of themselves is intimately related to their understanding of their culture and background, these ideas are also important in other sections of this book (see A5, *Valuing and respecting differences between people)* and, as a positive self-concept is so important for children's ability to learn, (see D, *Playing and learning).*

Andrew (7 months) with Vicki

Andrew selects a box from the treasure basket*, it is a small cardboard box with a brightly-coloured flowered pattern on it and he sucks on the corner of the box. Vicki notices as she brings Daniel over and says to him, 'Oh, Andrew, you're sucking on that box. There you are, Daniel, let's go over to Andrew.' Daniel and Andrew are at the treasure basket together and they seem to be talking together for a moment. *Vicki knows how important*

1.1 Adults understand the importance of each child's developing self-concept and self-esteem, understanding the role of social interaction and adult expectations in their development

Adults help children to develop a positive self-concept and appropriately high self-esteem by doing things together, encouraging them and praising them for their effort and their achievements and by giving them opportunities to do things they feel proud of. This is based on firm foundations when adults get to know children well, taking care to learn about their individual likes, dislikes, and interests. It also helps children to feel good about themselves when they know that their *children's names are. She uses Andrew's name positively, to get his attention and then uses it again, as she introduces Daniel – again by name. She also tells Andrew that she has noticed what he is doing. She can convey by her tone of voice and her body language that she approves of what he is doing – she knows that he is not trying to eat it, but exploring it with his mouth.*

Rachel

'I have noticed that some children just give up if I get a bit cross or impatient – like when the older ones need to get their shoes on to go out in the garden. But when I sat patiently by Finn and encouraged him to do up his own velcro, he managed really well. He went running off saying to everyone he met, "I managed! I managed!"'

Rachel got her expectation of Finn just right: with her support and encouragement he was able to do up his own shoes and he was appropriately proud of his achievement, and of his growing independence. This little episode also shows how important it is to give children time, which is often in short supply in a busy nursery.

special adults feel good about themselves and their achievements.

Nursery staff can feel proud of their children's achievements. They can take a real professional pride in a child's walking or his growing ability to wait a moment or to put words together. It is very important for children to have their efforts and their achievements noticed and recognised. It gives them feelings of success and confidence, which enable them to risk more learning. Talking and listening to children in an interested and accepting way can make as much difference as smiles and hugs or the words, 'Well done!'. For babies, simply imitating back to them what they have just done lets them know their achievements are valued.

Adult expectations have a big influence on children's self-concept; it matters very much how adults view the capabilities of the children in their care. Do they notice all the things a one-year-old *can* do, or all the things he *can't*? Are they looking for his competence or his incompetence? As we tend to find more of what we are looking for, looking for incompetence is discouraging for children. On the other hand, expecting far more than a child can manage is bound to result in failure for the child and he may give up trying. As a child grows, adult expectations need to be – like Baby Bear's porridge – not too high, not too low, but just right.

The names children are given, and the way they are used, tell them a lot about how other people see them. These names can confirm a child's confidence, or threaten it. An affectionate nickname, lovingly used, can help a child feel good, whereas nicknames like 'Trouble' and 'Misery' give a child mixed messages. Often, the tone of voice is more important than the actual name. 'Come on, Terror' said in a loving way, can be more positive than 'Come on, Clever Clogs' in a 'putting down' voice. A child may have a nickname at home which he and his family are happy to have used at nursery, but it is always a good idea to check and discuss these things, because names are so important.

Children very much enjoy it when adults put their name into a familiar rhyme, song or story, or use it in games like 'Peepaboo'. Home-made books also help encourage their interest in themselves and their special adults, as can looking in a mirror together. It all helps them to feel known, enjoyed and important.

Songs, rhymes and games offer lots of opportunities to enjoy doing things together. Adults can help their children feel good about themselves and their abilities simply by doing things together – especially the things which the children like to do most.

KEYPOINTS

- Children learn about themselves through their relationships with others.
- Adults can help children feel good about themselves simply by doing things together.
- Adult expectations are important, as are the names children are given.

1.2 Adults are aware of children when they are on their own and sometimes respond by actively leaving them in peace, whilst still remaining aware of them

Children on their own might be lonely and forgotten, anxious and unsure. Equally, they might be relaxed and happy, lost in their own thoughts, or totally absorbed in investigating something interesting. Children in nursery spend a lot of time watching and wandering. Watching what goes on and, for mobile children, wandering about from place to place and person to person, often comes before settling down to one activity. Of course, children who are free to wander about have many more opportunities to explore than those placed in a bouncer or playpen.

When they seem to be absorbed in an activity, which might mean just watching carefully, children may welcome a friendly question or a running commentary on what they are doing, but they will not want to be

Sarah (14 months) and Chris

Sarah is by herself. She moves again to the table, takes some more cornflakes and then looks up at Chris, who is showing Charlie the mobile. Sarah gurgles with pleasure and smiles broadly at the mobile and then moves back to the cornflakes, eats a few more, returns to her beanbag, crawls on her tummy and rolls over and onto her back, in a sort of big flopped out movement. She rolls round and round on the beanbag and then goes back to the rocking boat. She climbs into the boat by herself and rocks herself.

Sarah is on her own, but checks back with Chris, who is her key worker. It is important to be aware of what children are doing

on their own. Chris can learn a lot about Sarah by watching what she does at times like these. What is she interested in? How is she feeling? What is she thinking about?

Kimberley (7 months) with Lara

Kimberley is left by herself. She is delighted to find herself in the mirror – she laughs at herself happily and she plays peepaboo in the mirror with herself. She is vocalising and gurgling to herself. Lara says to Kimberley, 'Hiya!', and she joins in the mirror game with her and laughs with her. Kimberley seems to have initiated this interaction by her joyful and engaging behaviour. *Kimberley has spent some time very happily on her own, looking at a mirror. Lara comes back to her and joins in her game, laughing with her. What could be better for finding out about yourself than a mirror and an adult to help you enjoy what you can do with it?*

David (21 months)

David … tips the whole bath of ribbons out onto the floor … He then takes a run at the ribbons exuberantly and rushes at the texture and rustle of them. David finds a doll and waves it around and throws it into the middle of the ribbons and then he throws himself after the doll and on top of the ribbons. He pretends to sort of swim in the ribbons, lying on his tummy. He makes swimming movements and is playfully exploring the ribbons. *The adult has set up a bath full of ribbons and then stepped*

whisked away to do something else. Children in nursery are often interrupted in what they are doing by nappy changes or out of a concern for safety. A child who is interested in climbing, for instance, may find himself whisked away from those fascinating steps again and again!

Children's time alone can be valuable. It helps their learning and their self-esteem if their interests can be recognised, supported and given time and space. It can therefore be very helpful for staff to be aware of a child doing something on his own, but decide to leave him in peace to get on with it. This values the activities which he has chosen himself.

Times such as these offer staff excellent opportunities to observe a child carefully and learn more about what makes him 'tick'. If a child's interests are inconvenient or dangerous it may, on reflection, be possible to offer alternative ways to pursue them. It is very helpful if adults can make an activity safe or provide an alternative which feeds the same interest, for instance, providing a keen button pusher with a replica phone (or at least a disconnected one!).

When children wander about, they often go to places of comfort and rest: a favourite chair, cushion or corner, frequently chosen with a view to being less visible to the adults. Given the opportunity, young children often choose to be alone with a book. They may like to choose one – an old favourite or something new – and settle down with it in a cosy place.

Once they can move, babies will crawl or shuffle over to a book box, choose some, mouth them, lift flaps and turn pages. (This is based on lots of enjoyable experience of sharing books with adults and other children.) Again, adults need to distinguish when to leave a child alone, and when to offer to join in. Time alone with a book can be a valuable chance to recharge the batteries, before re-engaging with other people and things.

back and let David explore them alone and in his own way. He enjoys them as a whole body experience!

KEYPOINTS

● Children need time to watch and wander about.
● Children's time on their own can be valuable for their learning.
● These times are good opportunities to observe children

Conclusion

There are many ways in which adults can help children develop a positive self-concept. The main way is by understanding its importance and the role of social interaction in its development. Adults can make sure children know that they are interested in them, enjoy their company, like doing things together and recognise their achievements. They can have appropriately high expectations of the children – not too low and not too high. They can be careful about the names children are given and use their positive power. They can also be aware of the value of times a child spends alone, pursuing his own interests.

QUESTIONS FOR REFLECTION

● How do children learn who they are?
● How do staff develop their expectations of children with special needs?
● How are children's names valued and used in the nursery?
● What do children understand if they hear themselves described as 'a real lad' or 'a pretty little thing'?
● What do children like to do on their own?
● How often do you find that you have to interrupt what a child is doing? Why?

2. Friendships

Babies are intensely interested not only in their important adults but also in each other. They have a seemingly inbuilt desire to communicate, to use sound, touch, visual signals and shared play to initiate and sustain relationships. This element of the framework indicates ways in which adults can encourage, support, sustain and enrich the relationships young children wish to make. There are many ways adults can help; the three kinds of support chosen will make a positive difference to children's experiences of making relationships with each other.

The capacity for forming relationships is visible in the first weeks of life and established in the first year – but there is still a lot to learn. The strategies and skills children need for initiating, maintaining and enjoying relationships with others include: appreciating another's point of view, supporting others and understanding other people's attitudes and feelings, taking turns, problem-solving, negotiating – all in a wide variety of contexts. These are skills which we continue to develop over our entire lifetime. Most adults would also like children to develop a range of strategies for solving conflicts in peaceful ways and a perception that peaceful ways are best.

Adults can, by their active presence and skilled intervention, help young children learn these important skills and enjoy their relationships with others, including their siblings and their friends outside nursery.

Aisha (23 months)
Aisha sits down to breakfast with four other children just after 8.30. She chooses her cereal and is still enjoying it (at 8.48) when a boy of about two and a half arrives, kisses his mother goodbye and announces 'I want to sit next to Aisha'. She seems quite content at this

2.1 Adults recognise and value children's developing friendships with one another

There are many things adults can do to recognise and support children's developing friendships. When adults are aware, through observation, of who seems to like whom, they can make little adjustments to support the friendship, almost without thinking about it. They may simply move a chair so that a child can

suggestion, (and) H. quietly rearranges the chairs so that the newly-arrived boy can sit at the table next to Aisha.
This tiny incident shows the adult's commitment to foster children's friendships – she simply moves a chair, so two children can sit together.

Andrew (7 months), Joe and Sophie with Vicki

Joe is frightened by a car alarm that goes off outside and makes a terrifying squeal. Sophie (another child) pats Andrew's head comfortingly as she notices that Andrew is disturbed by Joe who is upset ... Vicki notices Sophie attentively patting Andrew on the head and she says to Sophie, 'Is that your friend Andrew? Are you playing with your friend Andrew?'
Sophie, who can't be older than three, is sufficiently tuned in to Andrew's reactions to know that he has been frightened by Joe's squeal. Vicki, the staff member, notices and comments on Sophie's friendly concern for him. It would have been even better if Vicki's comment had been something like, 'Are you comforting your friend, Andrew?'

sit next to his friend, or bring an extra mat so that two friends can settle down for their sleep together.

Adults can also encourage young children's interest in others by talking to them about what other babies and children are doing. They can also help by talking to them about how another child is probably feeling – this helps them begin to think about how other people feel and think. Adults can bring children's siblings and friends outside nursery into the conversation; these are important people in a child's world.

When very young children want to make a relationship with another child, they will often use physical contact to communicate. They will not, as we often do, exchange remarks about the weather! They use and enjoy physical play. Tumbling and romping like lion cubs is 'age-appropriate behaviour'. Sometimes, adults intervene as a matter of habit in the game, fearing it will get out of hand, noisy, disruptive. It is worth pausing and asking, ' Is this really aggressive and one-sided or actually friendly, affectionate and mutual?'

On the other hand, in seeking to nurture friendships, it is also important to recognise any real antagonisms between children; after all, friendships can be nurtured, but they cannot be forced.

KEYPOINTS

- Babies are intensely interested in each other.
- Adults can help children feel good about themselves simply by doing things together.
- Adults can help children develop friendships by helping them be together and by talking about other children, including their siblings and friends outside nursery.

Sarah (14 months)

Sarah is still busy with the books – she has a whole heap around her now and she is laughing with pleasure as they almost emptied the book rack around her. Sarah really loves this session – she is very enthusiastic.

Sarah talks through her dummy and Chris says to her, 'You have read every single book, Sarah!' Then Chris makes a big pile of the books and it is turning into a sort of give-and-take game – Sarah offers a book and Chris takes it. She loves this to and fro handing the books to each other and Chris is talking with her all the time.

With Chris near her, Sarah has been enjoying handling heaps of books. Chris acknowledges and values what she is doing and Sarah starts to offer more and more books to her. Chris accepts and encourages this enjoyable game, offering lots of talk too. They are enjoying being with each other.

2.2 Adults accept and encourage children's give-and-take games

Children's give-and-take games start with the give-and-take of looks, facial expressions and little noises between infant and mother, and lead up to the early symbolic exchanges of gifts in give-and-take games, and the little messages and elaborately wrapped parcels of older but pre-literate children.

Give-and-take games are not just fun, they are an important way of striking up and developing relationships with other people. They may also have significance for children's development of literacy skills (sending and receiving messages) and the development of speech (taking turns in conversation).

Providing a variety of treasure baskets* creates lots of opportunities for give-and-take games. As part of their interest in each other, babies will choose and offer objects to other babies, accept them, reject them, ask for alternatives etc – all without spoken language.

Adults can support and enrich these early exchanges. This support may just consist of being near and being aware of what is happening. Babies will feel good about what they are doing when they know adults recognise and approve. Then they will do more of it and develop their ability to communicate with others.

KEYPOINTS

● Encouraging give-and-take games helps children develop friendships and communication skills.
● Just being near and being aware helps.
● Treasure baskets provide good opportunities for give-and-take games.

Ross (24 months) and Terry

Ross is playing with his friend Terry with bubbles in the water. They froth, scoop and splash with the funnel. There is sustained conversation between the children about a hole that the

2.3 Adults enable children with shared interests and schemas to enjoy playing together

One way to support children's ability to develop and sustain friendships is to enable children with shared interests and play patterns (schemas*) to play together.

water is flowing down and into the trough … There is much discussion between these two children, they play companionably with shared pleasure in the flow of the water over the ridge. They are laughing together at the effect of pouring the water and increasing the flow … Their talk includes the following, 'Water, water, dry water, bang, bang, bang, it's water, I swim', with much reinforcement of gestures and actions to accompany the things that they are doing in the water. *Ross and Terry are enjoying playing together with the water because they are both interested in how it behaves and they are free to explore its possibilities. As they are learning about water, they are also learning about friendship, expressing and sharing their pleasure with laughter, talk and gesture. It helps when adults acknowledge this learning – even if the floor does get a bit wet!*

Leila

'They push and pull and grab. They have a language of their own. They copy each other, make noises together, point, chase, giggle, laugh at books together, hide together, get jealous, fight …

Leila is speaking about two children of 14 months, who are clearly very interested in each other and in doing things together – including sharing books – and all this before spoken language! It helps when adults enable children with shared interests to have time to play together – which may just mean settling two children with a selection of picture books.

Their shared interests and preferred play patterns make a good context in which to enjoy each other's company and develop their social skills. Finding a friend who shares an interest also nourishes it, which helps children's intellectual development.

The first step is to get to know individual children really well, by observing their behaviour in nursery and by talking to parents about what they like to do at home (see C2, *Staff–parent relationships* on p.67). It may be that there are two children with a passionate interest in trains and joining bits of track (connection schema*), or in wheels and rolling (rotation schema*), or both!

The second step is to think about how nursery activities and resources are organised and how staff decide who does what, when and with whom. For instance, when it comes to deciding who has a turn in the water tray next, staff often consider that taking turns and sharing are the priorities. It may be of more benefit to consider offering individual children time and opportunities to play with someone who shares their interest, for instance, in water wheels (rotation schema). This can also be effective as a behaviour management strategy.

Adults need to be realistic about very young children's abilities to take turns and wait. Before active cooperation is possible, young children will enjoy parallel play – playing alongside but not together – very much aware of the other but with little direct interaction. Staff can support parallel play and minimise unnecessary conflict by providing enough similar playthings. They can also help by offering a commentary on what a child is doing as a support for his interest and a 'bridge' to share that interest with another child. Children who share an interest have a lot to enjoy and talk about together – so their language development will benefit too.

KEYPOINTS

- Adults can help children with shared interests and schemas* to enjoy playing together.
- This can help children's social and intellectual development.
- Parallel play comes before active cooperation.

Conclusion

Adults have an important role to play in supporting children's growing ability to communicate with each other and form friendships. It helps children to develop the skills needed if the adults recognise the importance of these friendships and of the give-and-take games they use to build them. Children will also be supported by being offered opportunities and time to play with children who share their favourite play patterns, special interests and enthusiasms.

QUESTIONS FOR REFLECTION

- How do you know when two children are developing a friendship?
- Are you aware of individual children's friendships? How do you support them? When do you intervene?
- How can children with shared interests and enthusiasms be helped to play together?
- To what extent is learning to share and take turns important?

3. The group and the individual

Being part of a group, and the nursery as a whole is a very large group for a small child, is a valuable opportunity to try out what is later called 'citizenship'. There is a lot to be learned about being part of a group and conforming to the group's expectations. It takes a lot of experience to realise that, when you put your own needs second to those of the group, you get a feeling of participation and a sense of belonging.

Daycare settings offer children many more opportunities to experience groups than they would normally experience at home: groups for sharing food, sharing stories, songs and rhymes, and even sharing sleep and times to go to the toilet.

It makes a big difference how adults handle these opportunities to learn about being in a group. Group times can be organised and handled in such a way that children learn about the pleasures of sociability and participation, as well as about conforming to adult expectations and rules.

This element of the framework is based on the conviction that participation in a group is a valuable thing. It identifies three aspects of the adult's role which can enhance the children's experience of belonging and contributing to a group.

Georgia (31 months) with Kat

Georgia watches Kath's actions and sounds (as she does 'Katie hammers with one hammer') and listens as she says, 'We like this one'. Georgia nods to her in agreement. Georgia joins in with hammer movements with her arms and nodding head movements. She then decides to shout out very loudly in one of the quiet sleepy bits. Kath ignores her and Georgia notes this lack of response and so resumes the actions and clapping of the song. Kath

3.1 Adults support children's growing capacity to participate in a group

Adults can do a lot to support children's growing but very variable capacity to participate in a group. They can establish the ground rules of a group situation and explain them clearly and apply them consistently and kindly. It helps if children are clear which bits of an activity are negotiable by individuals and which bits are not. Adults can set up routines and give clear signals about when a group activity is going to happen. This helps children prepare themselves for what is coming, and gives them more of a sense of control about the situation.

notices that her behaviour is now fitting in with the rest of the group and she is joining in this shared activity and reinforces her good behaviour by calling her name as part of the song. Georgia smiles in response to this attention and enthusiastically stands up for the 'I'm a little teapot' song'.

Georgia has been struggling to participate in group times, such as this songs and rhyme session with Kath. As part of her group management strategy, Kath decides to ignore Georgia's negative group behaviour (shouting loudly in a quiet bit) and to reinforce her positive group behaviour. In this case, Georgia responds with enthusiastic participation.

In Ross' (24-months-old) nursery

9.55 The children are asked to sit and wait on the mat while the staff finish preparing and arranging the toys for the children to choose from. There is a choosing time ritual and Helen says, 'We will choose people who are sitting nicely, smart, quiet children.'

Adults are in a position of power over children and need to be careful how they use it. As part of her strategy for managing the group – keeping them seated while the staff put toys out – Helen puts her statement positively, but children who are finding it hard (and none of them are over three) might get the message that they are not 'nice, smart and quiet'. ('Quiet' is clear enough, but what do 'nice' and 'smart' mean anyway?) There might be better ways of managing this situation.

Adults can use their knowledge of individual children to adapt group routines to their needs and abilities. They can support their participation through the use of their name in songs and rhymes, and by carefully choosing songs and stories loved by individual children. They can sensitively help children pair up for 'Row, row, row your boat' and re-form again into a whole circle. These are definitely skills which children need to learn.

Adults can also help by being sensitive to children's varying needs for individual time, small groups and larger groups. In general, children become ready for larger groups as they grow older. However, even tiny babies can be part of large group happenings if they are happily on a familiar carer's lap, just as babies enjoy going to group activities with their parent but would hate to be plonked on the floor and left! But some days, an older two-year-old who normally likes the nursery's sociable toilet time, may just find the large group too much. It helps when carers are observant, and when nursery routines allow them to be flexible and follow the child rather than the timetable.

Conforming to the expectations of the large group can feel like a terrible tyranny to a young child. Children are often required to 'Sit nicely and wait for your turn'; they have to share adult attention and accept other people's choices over their own. This is why children need support which is sensitive to the struggles involved.

It is worth thinking carefully about children's experience of group times. Are they learning more about obedience and conformity than about participation? What kind of behaviour receives praise? What kind is rejected or ignored?

KEYPOINTS

- Children need sensitive support to learn to participate in a group.
- Adults help by establishing the ground rules, but being aware of individual needs and abilities.

Ross (24 months)

(Ross) holds hands with Shannon and they then get into the right position for the next rhyme which is 'Row, row, row your boat'. The large group of children all join in... . There is a lot of screaming at the end and Ross pinches his cheeks in excitement and looks at all the happenings with the other children.... Ross lies down for the last song, which is a quiet number to conclude with. He is lying next to Shannon this time and he plays affectionately with Shannon's hair ... They both join in the familiar routines of the lines together. They seem to know in unison when to jump up, when to lie down, when it is time to run round the room, when it is time to scream.

Being next to your friend is a great help in knowing when to scream! Staff need to appreciate that young children communicate with each other physically, while bearing in mind their nursery's child protection guidelines. If staff ever feel uneasy about children's behaviour towards other children or themselves, they should talk to their line manager.

Georgia (31 months)

Georgia dismounts from her bike and goes to lie underneath the slide ... Paul joins her and they both lie on their tummies together under the slide, snuggling up and romping and rolling around together.

This is a typical example of young children's friendly communication without words.

3.2 Adults understand and value the variety of ways in which children communicate and behave in groups

Children communicate and behave in a variety of ways in groups. They communicate physically, with gesture and with their whole bodies, as well as using a whole repertoire of sounds. They may experiment with clicking sounds, drumming their feet or roaring like a lion. Other children may respond by copying what is offered and returning it, often magnified for good effect. This can be tricky for the adult seeking to manage the group, but it is best understood as ways children communicate in groups rather than defiance (although it may be that at times!)

Children show their delight in each other's company with laughter and humour. Their joke may be that one child has made a sound by tapping the floor with his feet and another has done the same. This kind of shared humour helps children establish the feeling of being in a group. If adults understand and value the variety of ways children communicate and behave in groups, they can balance, for example, the adult desire for good manners at meal times with the opportunity for a little child-like fun. An important part of a songs and rhymes session is sharing the whispery quiet bits and anticipating the release of the scream to come!

One way for children to cope with being in a large group, if they are finding it a bit overwhelming, is to make themselves part of a smaller group within it. Sitting next to a friend, maybe touching her and exchanging looks, can help, as with Ross and Shannon in our example.

Lots of children show how much they enjoy group times, rushing to find a place in the circle for a story or bringing a chair to a table for a group snack. As children grow in confidence in group situations, they may wish to experiment with switching role from the led to the leader. Playing orchestra games, where one child can be the 'conductor' and experience the power of leading all the others, is one way of offering this opportunity.

KEYPOINTS

● Children communicate and behave in a variety of ways in groups.
● They communicate with each other physically, with a wide repertoire of sounds and through shared humour and it helps when adults understand this.

Jo, key person for David (21 months)

'(David) needs to have his blanket. They all know who likes what in the nursery. David knows that H. likes her bunny and he will take her her bunny and vice versa, H. will bring David his blanket if he needs something. I think they're aware that they're each different and they each have different things that comfort them.'

Seamus (11 months)

Clare lifts him gently and returns him to the circle of children who are singing and having rhymes, but Seamus is still not into the song session... Seamus claps with them momentarily and then walks to the sofa, then he walks back to the book, then he walks back to the rug to play with the car. Nicola then remarks to the other staff, 'Seamus is not singing'. Nicola's comment that Seamus is not singing is a relaxed and non-judgemental acceptance of the difference between Seamus and the other children on this occasion..

Nicola declines to be locked into a battle of wills with him, which makes it more likely that, on another occasion, he will choose to join in with the group.

3.3 Adults encourage and support children in accepting and valuing individual difference

Nurseries provide group care, but the ethos of a nursery can either emphasise similarity or recognise and value the differences between children. Staff can consider as a group whether it is desirable for mattresses to be laid out in parallel rows, as in a hospital, or whether all the children should wear identical bibs and eat their food from identical bowls.

It is all a question of balance: children, like adults, will grow to appreciate the solidarity of the group, but need to be sure they are valued for what makes them unique. Unlike adults, children are only just beginning to learn about their identity, so it all feels much more fragile and likely to fall apart.

In some nurseries, recognition of individual difference is part of everyday life, acknowledged by adults and children alike. The children know about each other's individual comfort objects and, if they find someone else's on the floor, they will be concerned and look for the child it belongs to. After all, they know how important their special comforter is to them – they are showing their developing power of empathy in recognising its importance to someone else. Returning an object to its owner is also a way of making friendly contact, a version of the 'give and take' game.

Staff can also recognise differences in children's attitude to group times, choosing to tolerate and accept a child's non-conformity on a given occasion. As children grow older, expectations can be adjusted – again, it is all a question of balance.

Nursery planning can recognise or ignore individual difference and gives out powerful messages to children about what matters. The desire to 'give everyone a turn' (and for everyone to go home with a card for Mum) can often result in a hurried and puzzling experience which teaches them nothing positive either about participation or about how difference is valued.

Part of valuing difference is valuing individual children's choices. Being able to choose which underpants to put on after an 'accident' may enable a child to accept that he does indeed need to wear some!

KEYPOINTS

● Children can find some group experiences puzzling.
● It helps children to participate in groups when their individual differences are recognised.
● Nursery planning needs to balance the pleasures of being like everyone else, with the need to be an individual.

Conclusion

Children's experience of groups in nursery can give them pleasure and security. It can also be puzzling and difficult, as it involves the struggle between individual needs and group needs, the pleasure of being part of 'everybody' and the pain of letting go of being 'me'.

Adults can support children's growing capacity to participate in groups, understanding and valuing the variety of child-like ways they communicate and behave with each other.

At the same time as children are learning about being in groups, they are learning about being themselves – their developing identity. Adults are in a position of responsibility and power over young children in nursery and so they need to think carefully about what children are learning about the value of their developing individuality and of their participation in groups, and how they can support children in accepting and valuing their individual differences.

QUESTIONS FOR REFLECTION

- Why does it help if adults understand how children behave in groups?
- What do children learn from how group times are organised and handled?
- How can group times recognise children's individual differences?

C. RELATIONSHIPS: ADULT–ADULT

Introduction

Section C is all about the relationships between adults in the nursery. It has two elements: one about relationships between staff in the nursery, and the other about the relationships between staff and parents. Number one is about staff accepting that young children are very sensitive to the feelings of the people caring for them and being aware of the kinds of behaviour and attitudes they are modelling to the children.

Number two is about one of the most important relationships of all from the point of view of the child: the relationship between her parents and her carers. This element is about nursery staff working in partnership with parents: acknowledging that all parents want the best for their children; actively establishing positive relationships with parents and finding out as much as they can about children's family background; welcoming parents into the setting and sharing both their practice and their experience of the children.

1. Staff–staff relationships

Working with very young children is hard work, both physically and emotionally. Although it is responsible and demanding, it is not well-paid and continues to be regarded as low-status work. Good relationships with colleagues can be a great source of support and many staff interviewed in the study commented appreciatively about the value of working as a team.

Nursery staff are often under pressure. Just meeting the physical needs of a number of young children can seem like a never-ending task. Then there are the emotional demands. There are times when carer and parent alike, faced with a baby who won't be comforted or a toddler screaming with frustration, is tempted to join in, or at least wail, 'But what about *my* needs!'. In these sorts of circumstances, relationships between staff can be put under strain.

Poor relationships with colleagues are undermining, both for adults and children. Young children are very sensitive to the feelings of the adults caring for them. They will sense when adults are tired and distracted, or refreshed and open to new things. They will know if an adult is having a 'sense of humour failure' that day. They will also sense if their carers like and respect each other.

It helps when staff have adequate rest periods, a chance to sit in an adult-sized chair and to switch off from the demands of the children for half an hour. Staff need support from their line manager, a sense that their contribution to the setting is valued and that they are growing in skills and experience. They need opportunities to talk through issues as a staff team, along with appropriate opportunities for professional development (see D4, *Adult reflection and learning* on p.93).

**Andrew (7 months)
with Jan**

Vicki … says to Jan, 'Can you take Andrew now? I am going to change Lucy's nappy'. Jan says in a lovely welcoming open gesture, 'It would be a pleasure!'. She gathers up Andrew as if it was the most important and lovely thing she has had to do all day, which of course it isn't because he is being anxious and grumpy and she is really just trying very, very hard not to let Andrew's grumpiness make her feel grumpy and tense in return. *Andrew is having a difficult day and Jan knows that she mustn't let Andrew sense any reluctance on her part to take him from Vicki, or he'll only get sadder and grumpier. She also knows that as a childcare professional, she has to manage her own feelings.*

1.1 Adults accept that young children are very sensitive to the feelings of the adults caring for them

Even the youngest baby is sensitive to the feelings and mood of the adults caring for her. While being fed, she will sense if her carer is tense and irritated or relaxed and warm. She will know if her carer is enjoying the closeness of the feed and giving it (and her) her full attention, or if she is distracted, her mind on the next thing she has to do or if she is anxious about what is going on behind the sofa.

Babies and young children know all this because they can 'read' adults' body language and tone of voice. They are also exquisitely attuned to facial expression. A mismatch between what someone is saying and their body language is disconcerting for a young child. For instance, a young child will be confused by an adult saying something comforting, but in a tense way.

Children will pick up on any tensions in the team. In their own way, they will know about the rota problems caused by staff absence and they may be particularly fractious and unsettled on precisely the days when the staff least need it! Conversely, the children will benefit enormously from the feeling given off by a settled team, who respect each other and enjoy working together. They will be aware of the good-humoured banter that goes on in a happy setting and notice when staff show concern for each other.

As babies and young children are so sensitive, staff need to be very careful about their own desire to chat to colleagues while in the nursery. While children love language and are happy to be chatted to, it is not appropriate for staff to talk 'over the heads' of the children, let alone gossip about children, their families or other staff. The talk young children enjoy and need most is one-to-one and about *them* and what they are doing.

KEYPOINTS

● Babies and young children sense the moods of their carers.
● Both children and adults benefit from the feeling given off by a settled and happy team.
● Young children like chat, especially when it is about them.

Rachel

'We do have definite roles, and we take turns for some of the jobs, but we have to be flexible. For instance, I was supposed to set up the lunches today, but Leah's been unwell and has literally been clinging to me all morning, so Jane said she'd do it, if I read Ollie, Leah and Tamara a story. Of course, I'll help her out with something else when she needs it. You've got to be flexible and it certainly helps to keep a sense of humour in this job! Although of course you try not to bring your home troubles to work with you, there are times when you know someone's got some problem. Julie (our supervisor) will always try and let someone, say, go an hour early to sort something urgent out. We know how hard it is to get the rota to cover all three rooms, so we'd never try it on!'

1.2 Adults model good humour, sensitivity and cooperation in their own relationships, acknowledging also when there are difficulties.

Modelling is a powerful tool for supporting children's learning. As children are sensitive to adults' feelings, and extremely observant about adult behaviour, they learn a lot from what they see of staff – both the good aspects and the less good ones! After all, many a parent has been brought up short by seeing their two-year-old wagging an accusatory finger, giving their teddies a good ticking off. They have also experienced a pang of pride to see their child open the door to friends with a smile and offering them a 'nicecupotea'.

Nursery staff are in an excellent position to model positive behaviour and attitudes to the children. They can model good humour, sensitivity, tolerance and patience. They can model positive learning dispositions* such as curiosity, perseverance in the face of difficulties and skills such as problem-solving and cooperation.

They can also model respect for their peers and constructive ways of dealing with conflict. It helps when adults do this modelling loud and clear, being aware of the messages it is giving out. After all, what we *do* has much more impact on children than what we *say*. It is no good asking children to 'share nicely' if you are observed sneaking the last biscuit from the tin yourself. You will have modelled something entirely different! (Unfortunately modelling works equally well for both desirable and undesirable behaviour.)

There will inevitably be difficulties within any group of people working together, especially under pressure; what matters is how any difficulties are handled. Problems in staff relationships can be both a result and a cause of high staff turnover. This is disruptive and unsettling for adults and children alike. Both will feel better in a settled, positive atmosphere where mistakes are allowed and seen as opportunities to learn something.

Supportive line management can help a lot in creating a culture in which it is possible for all staff, from the supervisor to the temporary nursery assistant, to view difficulties and problems as opportunities for learning and feel confident about tackling them together.

KEYPOINTS

- It helps children greatly when adults model good humour, sensitivity and cooperation in their own relationships.
- Adults and children feel better in a settled atmosphere where mistakes are allowed and viewed as opportunities for learning.

Conclusion

Children are very sensitive to the feelings of the adults caring for them and they will benefit from a positive atmosphere in a nursery and be adversely affected by a negative one. Staff are in an excellent position to model the ways of relating they wish to foster in the children through their own relationships with colleagues.

There is a major issue for line managers around providing staff with enough support, rest and ongoing training to do this demanding work. Staff, and therefore children, will benefit from greater opportunities for professional and career development than are generally available in the daycare sector at the time of writing. (See D4, *Adult reflection and learning* on p.93.)

QUESTIONS FOR REFLECTION

- What is it like to work in a setting with a positive atmosphere?
- What helps create positive relationships at work?
- Which behaviours and attitudes would you like to model to children? How can you do that?

2. Staff–parent relationships

Most nursery staff are very mindful of the responsibility and trust placed in them by the parents who leave their children in their care. They want to give the children they look after the best experience they can. One important way of doing this is through effective staff–parent communication.

Effective staff–parent communication can greatly increase continuity and consistency for the child as she moves between home and nursery; it can enable parents to feel confident that they know about their child's life at nursery; it can deepen the staff's knowledge of individual children – their home routines, interests, the significant adults in their lives, their cultural background and significant family events. This is valuable knowledge, which can then be drawn on in responding to that child and in planning activities and experiences for her.

Children's experience of daycare is greatly enhanced when staff and parents achieve not just effective communication, but working in partnership, sharing their concern for the child's well-being and their knowledge of her as she develops day by day. This helps young children to move more easily between their home life and their nursery life, as they sense that both their parents and their special carers know them and care about their well-being. As children are very sensitive to the feelings and attitudes of those around them, they are also greatly supported when they sense that their parents and their carers like and respect each other.

Rachel

'I have to say, when I first started working here I was in the Baby Room, and I did wonder about some of the babies doing such long hours, but as I've got to know more parents, and more babies, I've come to see that each parent makes the best decision they can. I haven't met

2.1 Staff acknowledge that all parents want the best for their children and support their choice to use daycare

All parents want the best for their children. Choosing to use daycare – particularly for a young baby – is a difficult decision, taken for a variety of reasons and it is re-enacted each day when the child is handed over to the nursery carers. It helps when parents know that a mum yet who doesn't want the best for her child. I find it's really helpful when we've got a good relationship, where we can say things to each other about what's going well, and what isn't. I remember once we had a mum who kept being late for pick-up in the evening. I explained to her how difficult it was for her child to see the other parents come and hug their children and take them home, and how difficult it was for *us*, trying to keep that child going until Mum came. I think she just hadn't thought what it's like at this end. She's better now – her boss lets her leave work ten minutes earlier. It's the small things that make all the difference.'

nursery staff approve of their child, and approve of them, and of their decision to use daycare.

Working in partnership with parents offers a positive perspective on the child's situation: her care is shared. Babies and parents deserve wholehearted carers, who are aware of the difficulties a child may experience being separated from her parents, but who are appropriately confident that they can meet her needs with sensitivity and skill.

The key person approach is very helpful here. Most parents are greatly reassured by the sense that there is a main person who looks after their child at nursery, and that they really know her and care about her as a growing individual. It is this knowledge which makes it possible for them to leave the child at all, and go to work.

However, both parents and staff can have very mixed feelings about children 'bonding' with their key worker. (See A2.2 and A2.3 in *Affection and attachment* on pp.21 and 23.) Many parents are pleased and relieved when their child 'bonds' with their key person and seems happy to be left with her, but it takes a truly confident parent not to feel a bit threatened by such a close relationship.

KEYPOINTS

● All parents want the best for their children.
● It helps when parents know that nursery staff approve of them and their child, and of their decision to use daycare.
● A key person approach is very helpful in working in partnership with parents.

David's mother (David is 21 months)

'He watches 'Thomas the Tank Engine' and he likes watching the metro go under the bridge … I think he is interested in the speed and length of trains. He likes joining the pieces of train together … if there aren't enough train pieces, he'll add on other things and if he can't make things long, he likes to make things tall – he piles all the cars up into a tall pile.'

David's carer, Leila

'David is very interested in trains, he has a 'Thomas the Tank Engine' hat. He likes to watch the trains … he knows the sound of a train, he likes the ('Thomas the Tank Engine' theme music). *Leila has talked to David's mother about his interest in trains (which also encompasses schemas about connection, speed, direction, length and height) and she offers David lots of opportunities to explore it at nursery too. This complements his experiences at home and helps his interest develop (see D1.2' Supporting children's interests on p.79).*

Vikram's father

They ask me about what kind of foods Vikram has at home … but I want them to look after their system – that is important and when I go home, I follow theirs … so I take note of what they have had at lunch too. *Vikram's father, like many nursery parents, is keen for his child to fit in with nursery patterns (which he calls 'their system'), and seems keen to alter their home patterns to fit in*

2.2 Staff actively establish positive relationships with parents and find out as much as they can about the children's family and other important adults, home routines, interests and cultural background

Most nurseries are aware, particularly in the early days, of the importance of finding out about a child's home routines and adjusting nursery routines to accommodate individual children. In the care of very young children small things, such as their own nappy creams and dummies, matter. Parents need a chance to talk about what matters to them about the way their child is physically cared for. Within a mutually respectful relationship, nursery staff can also explain their preferred practices. They could explain, for instance, why they would prefer to limit the use of dummies (or not use them at all).

It helps when staff find out from parents not just about home routines, but about children's interests. How does she like to play? What does she notice and enjoy? If parents and staff can share their knowledge of a child's interests, and offer opportunities for her to pursue them, her learning will be enriched, and is likely to be happy (see D1.2, *Supporting children's interests* on p.79). When parents and staff share their knowledge of children's play and learning, then parents will feel more involved in the child's life at nursery and therefore less 'cut off'.

When parents are encouraged to tell staff all about their child's 'important adults' – their parents, siblings, grandparents, the neighbour whom a two-year-old likes to kick a ball around with (and not forgetting significant animals) – conversations at nursery will be much richer and the child will feel she is understood. Staff can interpret 'gan-gan' as her very important grandmother who has a cat called 'Snowy', who will only eat fish, etc. Child, staff and parent all share a little piece of knowledge about something important to the child, which helps her feel understood and safe.

As part of their growing relationship with the child's family, staff will build up a picture of her cultural back-ground, which supports her developing self-concept.

with nursery. Partnership with parents ideally involves a two-way exchange of information to support a young child's well-being, with the possibility of some adjustments on both sides. Parents often comment on what they have been able to learn from their child's carers.

KEYPOINTS

● Children's well-being is supported when their carers find out about their home routines, their family, their interests and their cultural background.
● Home and nursery become complementary experiences when parents and staff share information about a child.
● Conversations will be richer and the child will feel understood and safe.

Georgia's mother (Georgia is 31 months)

'When I broke my arm I was in hospital, and she was very difficult then. She was playing up but they kept me informed all the time that I was in hospital on the phone. They would call me every day and they would tell me all the ups and downs, they would tell me when she was playing up or when she had a good day. They kept me in really close touch.'
During a difficult time, Georgia's mother really appreciated the nursery keeping in close touch about her, day by day.

Andrew's father (Andrew is 7 months)

'Alex has a way with him. She has what we call `strong cuddles' for putting him to sleep. She is firm with him and he seems to know that when she settles him down, that it is sleep time.'
Alex has shared her practice with Andrew's parents, which gives them a feeling of confidence in her. Andrew is a first child and his parents appreciate her experience and her knowledge of their baby. It is very helpful when staff share their experience of a child and

2.3 Staff welcome parents and carers into the setting and share their practice and experience of the children freely with them

Parents with children in daycare while they work can feel excluded from their child's life at nursery. There can be an underlying sadness about what they might be giving up as a parent, including seeing first steps and hearing first words and some might also feel a lack of confidence in their own parenting abilities.

The situation provokes all sorts of mixed feelings which can get in the way of staff sharing their practice and their experience of the children. Parents differ widely in their attitudes towards knowing what happens at nursery. Some seem to find it easier to trust their child to a nursery if they do it with blind faith, appearing not to want to know the details. Some are so appreciative that professional carers are prepared to look after other people's children that they don't feel they can enquire too closely into what actually goes on.

It helps when nursery staff are sensitive to these issues and actively welcome parents into the setting, sharing their practice and their knowledge of the child with them and encouraging parents to do the same, so that both parties can feel at ease when discussing a child's progress. Parents are often rushed when they deliver and collect their children, but these are key times of the day for communication between staff and parents. Developing a joint approach to handling the arrival and departure times can make a big difference to a child's experience of nursery. These transition times are important because it is then that a child has to cross the 'bridge' between home *manage to help parents feel confident about their own abilities.*

Sam's mother (Sam is 11 months)

'I've seen how they handle conflicts in the nursery and it has been a very important education for me, … When there is a conflict, they just acknowledge it with the children and explain why they mustn't do it and that works. It's different at home … but I try to do the same thing – I've been very impressed with what the nursery does.'

Sam's mother acknowledges what she can learn from the way nursery staff handle particular issues, in this case, conflicts between children. The nursery staff are acting as more experienced models for her in her own learning about children's behaviour and how to manage it.

and nursery and back again and the bridge can seem frighteningly wobbly for a very young child.

It helps when staff are confident about their practice and feel able to share difficult things, such as a child seeming unhappy, as well as good ones. Establishing positive relationships with parents also means that individual problems which arise, such as a child biting other children, or a parent being persistently late, can be dealt with more easily against a background of familiarity and respect.

Parents have much to learn from nursery staff and many will recognise this. Staff can model positive ways of managing challenging behaviour, for instance, or ways of introducing new foods. Another example is that parents can be surprised and impressed to learn how easily their child settles down to sleep in the nursery. Staff can feel good about sharing their knowledge and experience and become confident about explaining their practice.

There will be occasions when nurseries and parents have different needs and priorities. If positive relationships with parents have been established, then when differences arise between parental preferences and nursery policy, it is possible to discuss them together. It helps when all the staff know and understand nursery policies and are able to explain them to parents. Policies need reviewing regularly by the staff as a whole, preferably in consultation with as many parents as possible.

KEYPOINTS

- Parents with children in daycare can feel excluded.
- It helps when staff actively welcome parents into the setting.
- Arrival and departure times are very important.
- Establishing positive relationships with parents makes handling problems easier.

Conclusion

This section has briefly outlined some of the important advantages of nursery staff working in partnership with parents. Parents are experts about their own child; practitioners are expert about young children in general. There is a huge potential to support children's well-being when they work together.

Both have much to learn from each other. When parents and staff share their knowledge of a child and their concern for her welfare, it becomes a true partnership, and she is able to move confidently between them. When such a partnership can be achieved, it leads to confidence all round: confident staff, confident parents and confident children, and the child's experience of nursery is greatly enriched.

QUESTIONS FOR REFLECTION

- Why is working in partnership with parents important? What can get in the way?
- How do you welcome parents into your setting?
- How can busy parents be encouraged to make time to talk to nursery staff about their child?
- How much time and thought is currently given to children's important 'transition times'?

D. PLAYING AND LEARNING

Introduction

This section focuses on children playing and learning, and how adults can help them. It has four elements. Number one is about how adults 'tune into' children's interests and support their learning. It emphasises that children explore to learn, and have strong interests of their own, which are greatly supported by adult attention, understanding and skilled conversation.

Number two is about adults recognising and supporting children's communication and appreciating the value of songs, rhymes, stories and humour. It also looks at the ways young children begin to represent their ideas and feelings, and how adults can help.

Element number three is about providing a rich learning environment for the children, which feeds their interests, corresponds to their broad stage of development and reflects the breadth of their culture and experiences at home.

The final element, number four, is about providing a learning environment for the adults. It describes a way of working based upon reflection on practice and suggests the advantages of offering staff opportunities for accredited learning.

1. Supporting children's interests

This element of the framework is about how adults can 'tune in' to children's interests and support their early learning. Early learning is about much more than colours, shapes, numbers and letters, although when the time comes these will, of course, be important. It is also about more than acquiring physical skills, although these too are important for lots of reasons. Early learning is about exploring, discovering and solving problems, together with communicating and representing ideas, thoughts and feelings.

The framework as a whole is a way of seeing children and how adults can support them. Very young children are seen as active learners, busy being and becoming communicators, scientists, artists, users of signs, symbols and other expressive languages. Children, even tiny babies, bring thought, reason and feeling to their encounters with their environment and with other people. They are tremendously motivated to learn by exploration, with strong interests and a need to know why. Their desire to explore and learn can be greatly supported – or sadly held back – by the adults who care for them.

This element of the framework is based on ideas developed by the Russian psychologist Vygotsky*, who believed that young children's capacity to grow and learn can be encouraged and sustained by the attention of a more experienced person, usually an adult, who engages in dialogue with the child and provides appropriate experiences for him. The adult knows the child's interests well, respects him as a learner and follows the child's lead. With 'tuned in' conversation and well-matched provision, the adult assists the child to do, say, think and understand *with assistance*, what he will very soon be able to do *alone* (in Vygotsky's terminology, the 'zone of proximal development', that is, what the child is nearly able to do).

These ideas were later developed by Jerome Bruner and others into the concept of adults 'scaffolding' children's learning, that is, structuring and supporting their learning experiences, initially providing a lot of support and intervention, but gradually taking down the 'scaffolding' as the child is able to progress more independently.

Over the years, a number of different models have been developed for supporting children's learning and nearly all of them are based on adults observing and 'tuning in' to individual children in order to help them pursue their interests. Many practitioners have found a knowledge of children's schemas* profoundly useful, along with the concept of scaffolding their learning.

1.1 Adults support children's playful exploration of their environment, their ideas and their feelings

There are many ways in which adults can support children's playful exploration. One important way is by recognising that children explore to learn. Recognising and valuing children's exploratory play is really important. When staff focus on more than children's physical and emotional needs, and when their aspirations for children's learning are widened beyond such things as naming colours, children's opportunities for learning are greatly extended.

Children want to find out, discover, solve problems and communicate their ideas and feelings about what they are doing. In their play, they willingly grapple with big ideas like 'inside' and 'outside' or 'connecting' and 'disconnecting'. To help them in their adventure, they need the interested presence of a friendly adult who sees what they are trying to do.

Sometimes just being there is enough. Noticing children's play and staying with them really helps. Children under three explore through their senses – especially touch. Babies investigate new and interesting objects and materials by mouthing them, sometimes turning them over and over in their mouth, as adults might turn an unfamiliar object over in their hand or turn a thought over and over in their mind. They are exploring its properties: 'Is it hard? soft?

Alex about Andrew (7 months)

'He is selective. His personality is quite serious, not unhappy ... I would say he is quite intelligent and he knows what he wants, that is from home, I suppose? ... He does concentrate for a long time ... He studies things, you can see him thinking.'

Alex recognises and values Andrew's frown of concentration when he is thinking hard. At seven months, she sees him as a thinker and a learner. She knows what he is interested in: 'The treasure basket* is his favourite at the moment, he goes for all the stainless steel things ... He likes the pop-up toys, he likes to work it out' *She has observed how much he enjoys the Treasure Basket, and what he chooses most often. If she watches him carefully, she may be able to work out what it is about the stainless steel things he likes most: is it the feel of them, their temperature, their shininess? We can guess that what he is working on with the pop-up toys is the problem of cause and effect. Andrew is being a* *little scientist, investigating a sequence of problems: 'What happens when I do this? If I do it again, will it happen again? What happens if' etc.*

Sarah (14 months) and Charlotte

Charlotte sets the mobile in motion and they watch the moving pictures of Beatrix Potter together. Sarah reaches and Charlotte lifts her up higher so that she can reach the mobile and touch it.

They talk quietly together and then after a bit Charlotte puts her down, but Sarah continues to look up at the mobile hanging from the ceiling and Charlotte says, 'So you want to come up again?' and again holds Sarah up to the mobile. Sarah is really enjoying this and has another play before she is sat down. *Charlotte interprets Sarah's gestures and looks as expressions of interest, and gives her opportunities to explore by lifting her nearer to what she cannot reach herself. She also offers talk to support Sarah's interest.*

cool? warm? Is it smooth and round, or does it have sharp corners? Is it like anything else I have known?'. This mouthing behaviour can sometimes be misunderstood and discouraged. It helps when adults recognise this exploration for what it is and offer safe opportunities, for instance, a whole treasure basket full of safe and interesting things with varied texture and shape and weight.

One- and two-year-olds on the move are able to reach more and explore with their whole bodies. There is *so* much they are interested in. It is almost a cliché about children that they are more interested in the box a toy came in than the toy itself. This is because a large box, amongst other things, offers the opportunities to explore ideas about inside and outside, being hidden and being seen. A young child will explore such ideas physically, with his whole body. The box also offers slightly older children all sorts of possibilities for imaginative play.

Adults can help by creating opportunities: giving children the time and space for exploratory play. It helps when they resist the temptation to offer alternative activities or a new plaything too quickly. Learning often involves a struggle; it helps when adults can support children to persist and then experience the satisfaction of solving a problem. Children's learning may be hindered if adults are unduly concerned with safety and hygiene, putting them above all other considerations.

Exploratory play is driven by, and feeds, very young children's cognitive development. They appear to be driven to make sense of the world – what is in it and how it all works. They struggle with complex ideas, like whether an object is still there if you can't see it. Their brains are developing at a tremendous rate, processing all this new experience and forging literally millions of new connections between brain cells every day. Exploratory, open-ended play (what Tina Bruce calls 'wallowing') (Bruce, 2001, p.30) also offers children opportunities for exploring their feelings and their understanding of the situations and relationships they have encountered . This is the area of learning which has come to be called 'emotional intelligence'.

KEYPOINTS

● Children learn through exploratory play.
● Adults can help by giving children time and space for play.
● Noticing children's play and staying with them can really help.

Gloria about David (21 months)

'He likes wooden, clumpy things. He likes to hold them. He likes the watering can and pretending it's petrol at the petrol pump and he plays with that outside in the garden … he does make a beeline for certain things … this week, it's the wooden things but he also likes joining things together, that's one of the reasons I think he likes the trains.

Gloria has got to know David, observed what he is interested in and how he plays, and has been thinking about how his interests fit together. They are both making connections!

Andrew (7 months) and Vicki

Andrew plays with the cup and turns it round and over the tray, he makes his happy noises again. Jan takes the cup from him and Andrew rubs his hands over the tray playing with the bits of juice and food that were left behind from his lunch. Vicki comments, 'Are you having a lovely tactile experience with all that water!?'

Vicki observes what Andrew is doing, and interprets it as exploring to learn. She comments positively on his

1.2 Adults observe children's play carefully and seek to understand their interests and schemas

Most of all, adults can help by watching really carefully and seeking to understand a child's interests and intentions. Then they can respond to the child through 'tuned in' conversation and participation and, when the time is right, really engage in their play and their learning.

It helps enormously when adults have a sound knowledge of young children's interests. As they develop, most young children show interest in some of the universal schemas* (sometimes called play patterns), such as rotation, transporting things, covering things up and putting things inside, joining and separating things and trajectory (things which 'shoot' in a line, or an arc). Some older children will be interested in making web shapes or grids, while others will explore height and length in many different ways.

One- and two-year-olds are mostly very busy and 'into everything'. General knowledge about children's schemas forms a useful background for observing individual children's behaviour. General knowledge plus individual observations can reveal the theme that joins up all this busyness, the 'thread of thinking' (Nutbrown, 1994) that runs through it. Some children's behaviour is more obviously schematic than others.

Sometimes a child's behaviour can be puzzling. Staff who become confident about observing children can enjoy sharing their observations and puzzling together about individual children's interests and how to provide relevant *'lovely tactile experience', offering him language about what he is doing and interested in, rather than coming at him immediately with a flannel! It can help young children's language develop when their carers don't over-simplify their language, especially when it is in a rich context like this.*

resources and experiences for them. It is also very helpful to draw on parents' knowledge of a child's interests and 'obsessions'. (See C2.2, *Staff–parent relationships* on p.69.) There can be a real exchange as nursery staff who have built up a general knowledge about children's play patterns can shed light on puzzling (or inconvenient) behaviour at home, such as emptying all the waste paper baskets and tipping out drawers.

Understanding can lead to greater tolerance too: the pest who tips out waste paper baskets becomes the little scientist exploring ideas about 'what fits inside'. Once the interest is understood, it can also be more sympathetically managed: maybe the child would also be interested in putting all the waste paper back inside again and seeing if it fits? Or finding another waste basket to put it all into?

Sometimes it is really not clear what a child is trying to do. Good practitioners can tolerate not knowing and continue to wonder. By observing carefully and seeking to understand, staff model valuable learning dispositions.* (See D4.3 in *Adult reflection and learning* on p.97.) A positive attitude to learning is possibly the most valuable gift nursery staff can give to a child.

Georgia (31 months) with Marilyn
Marilyn is playing with the bricks with a group of children and Georgia goes to sit on her lap. They are building some towers together and she says, 'Getting bigger, hooray!' … Georgia sits happily on her lap and builds a tall tower of carefully and precariously balanced bricks. They are playing together: Marilyn offers bricks and lets Georgia choose where she is putting them. As Georgia builds up her tower, Marilyn is labelling the bricks: a big one, a triangle and she is describing the wobbliness of the tower. They laugh

1.3 Adults' responses are based on their knowledge of the child's interests and schemas*. Their conversations with children are matched to the child's interests.

Having observed a child's play carefully and learned something of his interests, adults can respond by being there, giving time, valuing his play and protecting it from others' interference. They can position babies who are not yet mobile where they can see or reach something interesting to them and offer them suitable resources. Best of all, they can 'tune in', and come alongside the children, engaging with them and their preoccupations.

Resisting the temptation to offer solutions to their problems or skills for them to imitate, adults can take cues from the children as to how best to support them in uproariously together with pleasure as they build a tower and select the different bricks that she is going to use ...

Marilyn has Georgia on her lap and supports her by validating her choices of bricks by describing their attributes and the effect of her choices on the structure as it grows. Marilyn offers bricks, but lets Georgia choose where she puts them. She fosters a conversation of words and gestures which matches Georgia's interests and her sense of humour. The tower building activity is sustained and enjoyed by both Georgia and Marilyn.

A parent

'Most of all she likes rhymes – she is not very good with toys, even at home. What she prefers is singing. She loves music and we have our own Bengali tapes – when she wakes up she goes straight to play this music.'

Parents know a great deal about their children's interests and it is very valuable when they are encouraged to share this knowledge with staff, so that they can provide appropriate opportunities at nursery. This sharing also helps children feel known and safe, and, as in this case, there are opportunities to include and value children's home experience and culture.

Andrew (7 months) and Jan

Andrew then pulls himself up on the sides of the (truck) he is sitting in and Jan responds, 'Where is Andrew going? You decide where you are going next'. She lifts him out, and he

what they want to do, nurturing their growing capacity to think, do and understand for themselves.

Most valuable of all, they can offer conversation matched to the children's interests. This conversation includes gesture and body language and starts with entering into the give-and-take games of babies. A real conversation has more than two turns, so that it has room to develop and there is a real exchange.

When done well, this conversation is very skilful work, involving detailed knowledge of the child, empathy, imagination, flexibility and humour. This is seen in our examples. Unspecific compliments ('That's lovely!'), instructions ('Put it back over there') or testing questions ('Where's the posting box?') are much less helpful for a child's learning than responses based on the adult trying to understand what the child is trying to understand ('hmm, I wonder if this brick will fit in here ... ') This is explained at more length in Goldschmied and Selleck, 1996. Similarly, hugs and tickling games can tell a child he is enjoyed, but not that he is valued as a thinker and investigator. (See *Ross and Tess* on p.85.)

When staff are 'tuned in' to children, it is easier to say 'yes' to what they want to do and avoid having to 'tell them off'. Not understanding what children want to do can lead to frustration on both sides. To make it worse, adults can then misinterpret children's growing distress at being misunderstood or prevented from exploring what they need to explore, assuming it is some kind of physical problem, such as hunger or teething pain. They may kindly but mistakenly offer food, drink, or a nappy change.

Sometimes, in a busy nursery, staff can feel a bit guilty about having a cosy five minutes sharing a book with a child on a sofa, or spending some time absorbed in water play with a child, when there are practical tasks to be done. However, five minutes of 'tuned in' dialogue with a child is more valuable for the child's learning and self-esteem than a dozen fleeting and superficial contacts. It supports children's learning when nursery organisation and culture encourage adults in the important job of engaging with children playing in the way which helps them most.

chooses to spin the wheel. Then Andrew has a look around at other things in the pool and Jan responds, 'Are you thinking about it, Andrew? I will let you think about it'. *When it isn't clear what Andrew is interested in doing next, Jan keeps chatting to him, but lets him think, not seeking to immediately interest him in a new toy, but giving him time and permission to think for himself.*

KEYPOINTS

● Supporting children's learning is skilled and valuable work.
● It helps children's learning when adults match their conversation to children's interests and take their cues from them.

Conclusion

This section of the framework, like all the others, is offered as a starting point for reflection. Sometimes the ability of children to play independently may be valued highly because it makes fewer demands on adults. Children *do* need time to explore independently (see B1.2, *Self-concept* on p.47), but they also benefit greatly from the presence of an interested adult alongside them.

In order to support children's learning, adults use their knowledge, perception and creativity. They, like the children they care for, also need the support of people slightly more experienced and knowledgeable, who value them as learners. In this challenging work, the understanding and supervision of a manager is enormously important.

QUESTIONS FOR REFLECTION

● Which of the models for supporting children's learning do you recognise? Which do you find most useful?
● How do you use observations of children in your nursery?
● Which schemas do you see in individual children's play? How can you support them?

2. Developing language and literacy

Young children try very hard to converse with adults. They want to communicate their thoughts and feelings and connect with others. They learn through exploration and conversation with interested others and they need to know adults are listening to what they are saying.

Real conversation with children is a skilled art. It works best when adults can abandon their own agenda and 'tune in' to a child's intentions, which are expressed in body language, facial expression, gesture and vocalisations (the sounds they make).

Children's language development and, later on, their literacy, are greatly supported by knowing and enjoying a wide repertoire of songs, rhymes and stories. Nursery staff can make these things a fun and enriching part of everyday life. They can also help by recognising and supporting the children's growing ability to represent their thoughts, feelings, memories and ideas.

Sarah (14 months) with Kate and Charlotte

... Kate talks with Sarah about the Beatrix Potter Peter Rabbit mobile, and they play an initiating, imitating game with each other. 'Ya, ya, ya,' says Sarah and Kate talks back to her. There is lots of vocalising between the two and then Charlotte responds, 'I think you're making "I want to come outside" noises. In a minute, in a minute.' Sarah then reaches for a toy and talks to herself ... And then she goes on to point at the mobile. Kate responds with lots of talking and Sarah vocalises in response to her.

Kate makes 'give and take' conversation with Sarah, imitating the sounds she makes. Kate makes their exchange into a conversation

2.1 Adults recognise and support children's early communication and respond by adjusting their own gestures, vocalisations and body movements to those of the child

The very first language is body language. Adults can recognise and respond to this language by responding in kind. This is the basis of many enjoyable conversational games with babies, which involve reflecting a baby's facial expressions, gestures and vocalisations back to him. He passes them back again or tries something different – and the game goes on.

This kind of game teaches the baby the art of making conversation. It also lets him know that he is recognised, his efforts to communicate are valued, and the adult enjoys doing things with him. Body language goes on being important even after spoken language has been mastered. As adults we continue to use it to check out what someone is really saying to us!

and helps Sarah sustain her interest in the mobile. Charlotte thinks about what Sarah is trying to say, interprets it and replies as if Sarah had been making sense. Sarah is learning a lot about how conversation works from all this.

Lesley with Sam (11 months)
Lesley continues to speak to Sam, stroking his cheek.
'He copies me now – you copy me now, don't you? [she smacks her lips at him] – yes, you copy me – clap your hands'. She continues to clap hands with Sam and he looks animated, holding his ears in a humorous, engaged way. Then as Lesley pretends to smack her ears, Sam mimics this.
Lesley and Sam are enjoying a copying game which develops into a give-and-take game, as she follows his lead by touching her ears. These good-humoured conversations without words will greatly help the development of Sam's language and social skills. They also help him to feel good about himself.

In conversation with children, whether in words, pre-verbal vocalisations or gesture and facial expression, speaking and listening are involved on both sides. It helps children to get the idea of a conversation when adults leave space for children to reply – a baby may take longer to reply than an adult. Listening is a valuable skill, which can be modelled very effectively by adults.

Babies and young children need to hear a lot of language before they can speak in words. They will enjoy a familiar adult chatting to them as if they were an older child, telling them what is going on, what is going to happen next, and bathing them in language. Most of all, they enjoy adults talking to them about *them* and what they are doing.

One of the advantages of group care for children is that there is a large pool of people to have conversations with. But conversation with young children works best when the adult is 'tuned in' to a child's interests and intentions. It is a skilled art and one that takes time and care.

No adult – even the most devoted parent at home all day with the child – could get their interpretations of a child's intentions and meanings right all the time. However, it is a missed opportunity for staff and a cause of frustration for a child if he repeatedly tries to make contact with adults to express his ideas and feelings and is met with incomprehension or misunderstanding.

Adults can help children distinguish the sounds in language by making sure there is not too much background noise, such as radio and recorded music. This is particularly important now that in many homes, one or more televisions are on all day. In a nursery setting, staff can also help by trying not to talk to each other 'above children's heads' or calling out to each other across rooms. It also helps when surfaces are soft and doors are shut quietly, so that children can concentrate on hearing one thing at a time, and aren't startled by loud and unpredictable noises.

Ross (24 months)

Ross seems very pleased to be part of this story session … (He) exclaims, 'A teddy bear!' (This is a familiar refrain which is part of the story) … Now Ross crawls round to the back of the group, and he joins in another routine about the three bears with all the other children. When they come to the bit about the porridge, Ross makes lots of sucky noises in the eating part. He is paying rapt attention even though there are all sorts of other things going on around him … Ross is completely focused on listening to the story.

Ross is engrossed in a familiar story, enjoying the predictablility of the refrain, the structure of the story, taking part in the ritual the nursery has developed for acting it out and adding his own sound effects for good measure. This is a rich and enjoyable learning experience for him.

Andrew's father (Andrew is 7 months)

'Vicki sometimes sings to him, there are two rhymes he specially likes … at home I sing 'Wheels on the bus' to him, this calms him too, but to be honest I picked that up from nursery too. We have learnt things from them.'

2.2 Adults appreciate the value of songs, rhymes, stories and humour and use them as part of their practice

Songs, rhymes and stories can be enjoyed as part of one-to-one and group interaction. When adults appreciate and use songs, rhymes, stories and humour, children learn so much to help their language development. Through songs and rhymes, tiny babies learn to enjoy movement and learn the meaning of 'up' and 'down', for instance, by experiencing them in a safe way with their whole body. They learn to anticipate what comes next and experience great satisfaction when it does! They gradually learn to co-ordinate their actions with the words and music.

Sharing stories helps children to explore familiar worlds and opens up different worlds to them. Children can get to know some stories really well. They can become old friends, to be enjoyed on one's own, with a friend or in a big group. Very young children can become passionately attached to a particular book, asking to be read it again and again and wanting to keep it by them. Some can become part of the shared fabric of nursery life. Well-known stories offer staff valuable opportunities for conversation around shared experience, as do favourite songs and rhymes. All this early experience of literacy will give the children a flying start at school later on.

Even very young babies enjoy choosing and investigating books, often with intense concentration. What do they feel like? How do they work? Which one to choose? There is a tremendous range of picture books available. Many for the youngest children offer richly coloured illustrations, textures, and flaps, quite apart from the variety and interest of the language itself. As their spoken language takes off, they often develop a hearty appetite

Familiar rhymes can become an enjoyable part of everyday life with young children. They can also help with routines like having a sleep or being strapped in a car seat, or introducing a change of mood or pace.

for new words, and show their enjoyment of the elements of language, such as rhythm, rhyme and alliteration.

Young children love it when adults share and value their growing sense of humour and appreciate their jokes. Truly 'tuned in' adults can enjoy daft substitutions like 'Humpty Dumpty sat on the cat' or putting a teacup on your head instead of a hat. When children enjoy this kind of humour, it shows that they have come to know something so well they can begin to play with it and that they are well on the road to literacy.

KEYPOINTS

● Sharing songs, rhymes and stories greatly helps children's language development.
● Babies enjoy choosing books and some stories can become old friends.
● Young children love it when adults share and value their growing sense of humour and appreciate their jokes.

Gloria about David (21 months)
'He throws things when he is in a temper, 'speaks' on the telephone … cuddles dolls and teddies, makes and talks about his Duplo vehicles, dresses up and acts out his ideas and feelings … '
Children represent their ideas and feelings in all sorts of ways – often through what they do.
Ross (24 months) and Tess
Ross makes a Sticklebrick candle, a long piece to represent the candle and another short piece fixed on the end to represent the flame. He pushes it into a large flat brick which (represents) the cake. Tess says, 'Look at that cake, put another one on'. Ross is blowing out the flames

2.3 Adults support children's developing ability to represent their ideas and feelings in gesture, vocalisation, mark-making, construction and imaginative play

Very young children represent their thoughts and feelings in what they do. As they explore, they begin to represent. The patterns in their play can point us towards the patterns in their developing thinking. A child interested in the 'connection' schema*, for instance, may connect and disconnect two poppers again and again, concentrating intently. Another child may pull a teddy repeatedly through the bars of a cot. As he is also fascinated by the gate across the doorway, is it possible that he is representing his ideas about boundaries and the possibilities of going through them? We can only find out more by watching carefully.

Children often need to repeat their investigations and their representations. Only by repeatedly getting in and on the candles. Helen and Tess join in his play and they sing 'Happy birthday' to him. Tess asks, 'Ross, do you know what you've got for your birthday?' Ross mouths the brick thoughtfully with his lips and then adds his 'candle' to his 'cake'. Tess tickles Ross in the ribs and says to him, 'Are you tickly?' … Tess shifts and Ross crawls off her lap. He takes the Sticklebrick with him and says to another child, 'I made that.'

In this example, Ross at 24 months is well able to use objects for representational play. Tess supports this play by recognising his meaning and she and Helen sing the appropriate song for him. After that, things go slightly awry: Tess asks him a question he cannot answer, and Tess resorts to tickling him. Ross crawls away. He shows he did not want to be tickled and diverted from his interest in the candles by saying to another child, 'I made that'. He wants his achievement to be recognised.

Chris about Sarah (14 months) painting
'She loves the variety of the brushes. She is not bothered with the painting really, but she loves the brushes. But the paint comes out of them. It was all over her hand but she wasn't bothered, she wanted more, she wanted blue. … They do what they want to do. … I don't help them actually make the painting, they do what they want, even if it goes all over the table. They are feeling the different textures of the paint.'

out of a box, for instance, can a child really get to the bottom of this 'in and out' business. They often use their whole bodies to represent their ideas. A child may, for instance, open and shut his knees when remembering the movement of an underground train's doors. This movement represents the memory of the movement which impressed him.

Adults support this kind of learning by watching carefully and trying to understand and respond to the child's interests and intentions.

It will be a long time before children are ready for more formal representation, such as painting a picture of Mum or making a card to mark an occasion. Given the chance, they will enjoy exploring craft materials such as paint and glue as things in themselves, but children under three are rarely ready to represent the idea of 'Christmas' on a card.

They will, however, enjoy experiencing new textures and seeing the marks they can make in paint or spilled food on a tray. The marks they make often simply represent, 'I was here – I did this!'. Their early experiments with paint and brushes are the trail of a gesture – the sweeping of a loaded brush across the paper. It helps when adults know that children are by and large much more interested in the process than in the product.

One- and two-year-olds can begin to use objects representationally, for instance, using a brick to represent a phone and talking into it, and they love to have a willing partner in their pretending game. However, babies who are offered a paper crown at a party are liable to rip them off their heads and mouth them, being unable to see what they represent. What they want most is a partner in the games they want to play – someone who wants to understand what they are saying and who laughs at their jokes.

Two-year-olds are often ready for fully-fledged imaginative play, acting out situations and trying out feelings and roles. They may also enjoy huge jokes, such as licking lollies made of Sticklebricks, and inventing flavours to try – some realistic and some outrageous.

Chris is clear that Sarah, like many young children, has her own agenda. They seem driven to explore and experiment. At 14 months, Sarah is not interested in making a picture – she is interested in the brushes and in the paint itself.

A 'tuned-in' adult will gamely lick an 'elephant' flavoured lolly in the name of supporting a child's developing power to represent his ideas and feelings.

KEYPOINTS

● Very young children represent their thoughts and feelings in what they do.
● They often need to repeat.
● Children's early marks may say, 'I was here!', but often the process is more important than the product.

Conclusion

When adults and children enjoy songs, rhymes and stories together, children catch the fun of language, its sounds and rhythms. Familiar books become old friends and new ones can open up unfamiliar worlds. When adults 'tune in' and respond to children's commun-ications, children learn how to talk and how to listen, and how to have a conversation. With support for their developing ability to represent their ideas in a variety of ways, children are well on the way towards literacy.

QUESTIONS FOR REFLECTION

● What helps you have conversations with children? When are good times to talk and to listen?
● How do you use songs, rhymes and stories with the children?
● How do young children express their sense of humour? How do you respond?
● How can adults support young children beginning to represent their ideas and feelings?

3. Providing a learning environment

Intentionally or unintentionally, planned or unplanned, a daycare nursery is a learning environment for children. Their learning is enriched when they are cared for in an environment that feeds their interests, corresponds to their broad stage of development and reflects the breadth of their culture and experiences at home.

Young children have no compartments in their learning and they learn from all their experience. The way the nursery environment is organised and resources are made available to them tells them a lot about adult attitudes to them as learners. They also learn from the attitudes and behaviour of those around them. Skilled staff who are able to 'tune in' to individual children's interests use not only play materials, but also the everyday opportunities of nursery life for talk and learning.

Children's learning is supported by being given time and space to explore open-ended materials, with an adult nearby who is interested in what they are doing and able to join in when needed.

Andrew (7 months) with Vicki

Andrew crawls over to more toys and then back to the green bottle again. He pushes it along and crawls onto the tiles and then over to Vicki. He rolls the bottle around the floor and then he changes to another bottle with pink fluid and energetically follows the bottle as it rolls across the lino. … He crawls off again onto the tiles and seems more active and involved in his play now, in fact he looks deep in thought … and Vicki comments, 'He's got that frown on again!' Andrew smiles and vocalises and she responds, 'Well done!' … (Vicki) protects Andrew's play and efforts to crawl and

3.1 Planning, organisation and provision of play materials are developmentally appropriate and responsive to the children's individual interests and needs

While play materials are sometimes used to amuse children and manage their behaviour, their most valuable function is to support children's learning and development. In order to do this, play materials need to be developmentally appropriate for the range of children in the nursery and they need to be responsive to children's individual interests, preoccupations and needs.

Open-ended play materials foster exploratory play which is potentially much richer than simply learning to master a toy which has a limited function. Open-ended play materials include sand, water, bricks and recycled materials such as tubes and boxes. Babies enjoy exploring a treasure basket of mixed or themed objects and materials. Open-ended play materials support a wide reach her. After a while she takes him on her lap again and they look at the postcard that Sophie sent the nursery when she was away on holiday. Andrew is interested in the postcard, turns it round and over and then starts to chew at the corner, but then begins to whimper. Vicki asks, 'Oh, are you bored again?'. She speaks with him some more. ... She wants to put him down but Andrew pushes up on his feet and seems pleased with himself again. Vicki says, 'He is saying, "Come on, let's have a wander".

Vicki considers what to say to him and what resources to offer him to match his preoccupations and remarks on his characteristic frown of concentration. She knows that Andrew is interested in wheels and the rolling movement of the plastic bottles with liquid in them (the rotation schema*). She also changes tack flexibly, as his interest shifts. She interprets his actions as representations of his thoughts. Using her knowledge of his interests at the moment, she could choose a rhyme or story he would enjoy and which would feed his interest in rotation.

Kath about Georgia (31 months)

'Georgia is absolutely mad about the water and taps, and exploring and controlling the tap flow of water. She loves to clean out with the mop, in fact she loves to help.'

Georgia is fascinated by the flow of water. Marilyn not only supervises but also adds extra

variety of individual children's interests and play at different developmental levels. When these materials are provided in quantity, they also offer opportunities for interaction between children, for being able to watch and imitate other children's play.

Children need uninterrupted time to explore these resources and they greatly benefit from an adult's interest in their play. If less emphasis is put on planning adult-led table-top activities, more adults are free to get down on the floor and join children in their spontaneous play, thinking carefully about how best to support it.

Flexible rotas for putting toys out can respond to children's interests and capitalise on their desire to learn. Once a staff team is confident about getting to know about children's interests, through observing them and talking to parents about their play at home, planning can start with the children rather than the calendar. Resources can be acquired or adapted to support individual children's interests – it is one of the great advantages of recycled materials that they are available cheaply through scrap schemes.

It also helps children's learning when they are involved directly in the choice of play materials available to them. Low shelving and boxes allow children to get out what they are interested in and even young children can learn to put toys and books back again when it is clearing up time – with adult support and encouragement.

Children need time to play and to develop persistence in the face of difficulties, including boredom. They can be overwhelmed if offered too many toys in quick succession, which can happen when adults are trying to 'cheer them up' or distract them from a problem.

Adult-led activities are best used sparingly with children under three. They will benefit from adult support in investigating an unfamiliar material, such as dough, if they are given lots of time to explore it firstly as a material. After this stage, they can be helped to investigate what they can do with it. Children may reject an adult's pre-formed idea of an activity, such as making three sausages from the dough to put in a pan, *resources such as tubes and funnels for Georgia to experiment with syphoning, blowing and tasting the water so that she can pursue her investigations. Marilyn also provides time and makes the most of learning opportuntities: she is unhurried when Georgia repeatedly flushes the lavatory, and elaborately wonders about the dripping taps in the bathroom. Marilyn and Doris talk to Georgia about the water and value her play in their adult conversations in the nursery. Marilyn also lets her help with the adults' work, allowing her to use the mop. Many of the richest play materials for young children are not 'toys' but everyday things.*

if it is offered too early and if it does not correspond to their own interest and ideas.

Similarly, when staff know that free play is children's way of learning, they see little sense in dragging children away from their chosen play activity to have their turn at something in which they have little interest. However, if they have, for instance, shown an interest in making their mark, they may enjoy trying an activity such as hand-printing, especially when a familiar and relaxed adult is supporting their experiments and discoveries. This is very different from a craft 'production line' in which all the children must take part.

KEYPOINTS

● The purpose of providing play materials is to support children's learning.
● Open-ended play materials support a wide variety of children's interests.
● Children need uninterrupted time to explore them.

Georgia (31 months) and Marilyn in the garden
Marilyn lifts her up even higher, so that they can both look over the wall of the garden together. ... I can see by Marilyn's gestures and Georgia's responses that they are talking about the leaves blowing off the trees at the end of the garden. ... Georgia is running at the end of the playground and excitedly watching the leaves spin down from the tree to the ground as the wind blows them off the branches. ... Georgia is having a very enjoyable, animated and exciting time catching the spinning leaves one by one. *Outdoor play offers children many valuable opportunities and experiences. The only way*

3.2 Adults provide a learning environment that is broad, balanced and non-stereotypical and reflects the cultures and experiences of children's families and communities

Aiming to provide a breadth of experience is particularly important in a daycare nursery, as children in daycare have fewer opportunities to experience the wider world outside than children cared for in a home setting, who may go out to shops and parks, to visit friends and neighbours or go swimming.

It helps children's learning when staff consider planning expeditions beyond the nursery walls and inviting in visitors with something interesting to share with the children. Outdoor play is so important it needs to be available every day. Amongst other things, it offers young children opportunities to explore earth and grass, sunlight and wind, the movement of leaves and the trails left by aeroplanes. It also offers the chance for *a child can learn about the wind is to experience it! Ideally, outdoor play is available every day, whatever the weather.*

Ross (24 months) with Helen
On the way (back from the nappy changing room), Ross and Helen have to pass through the entrance hall at the bottom of the stairs where there is a display of photographs of the members of staff. Ross stops there and he names all the staff on the wall with Helen.
A simple display of photographs of all the staff gives Ross the chance to refresh his memory of them all, and their names. Similarly, a display of all the nursery children – and even better – the children and their families – acknowledges the breadth of cultures included in a nursery. Where staff and children are in fact rather homogenous, it is particularly important to include images of a wide diversity of people and cultures.

a wider range of movement and for learning new physical skills. It offers play opportunities which are harder to provide indoors, such as building dens, and hiding and chasing games.

Another aspect of breadth is the variety of materials provided to play with. As so many bought toys, and children's equipment in general, is made of plastic, it is important to offer children other, more interesting materials to explore – some natural, such as wood and stone, and some synthetic, such as crinkly cellophane and glittering CDs.

Staff expectations of children are important. Staff can redress the pressure of stereotypical influences on children about gender, for instance, by expecting and encouraging exuberant and adventurous behaviour in both girls and boys, and respecting the needs of both sexes to observe and be apart at times. Staff can also make sure all children have clothing which does not restrict their play and think hard about how children at different developmental stages or who have special needs can be included in what is on offer.

In creating a rich learning environment, it is also important to draw on and reflect the cultures and experiences of children's families and communities. (See A5, *Valuing and respecting differences between people* and C2.2 in *Staff–parent relationships* on p.67.) Staff can work towards including each child's culture through song, dance, language, pictures, and playthings. This is helpful because it creates more continuity between home and nursery, as well as valuing individual children and their families and the diversity of people in general. Including a little wok in a range of cooking utensils in the imaginative play area, for instance, offers a reassuring continuity to a child who sees his parents cook with one every day. It invites him to participate. It also broadens the experience of all the children in the nursery.

Children are learning all the time, and skilled staff can make the most of everyday opportunities for talking and learning. These can arise from everyday routines and unexpected events, even minor disasters, such as a breakage or a flood under the sink.

> **KEYPOINTS**
>
> ● Outdoor play offers key learning opportunities for children.
> ● It helps to provide children with experiences of materials other than plastic.
> ● It is important for the nursery environment to reflect children's home cultures and the range of cultures in our society.

Conclusion

Young children learn and thrive in an environment full of things which allow them to explore their interests and schemas, and full of adults who are willing and able to support them in their explorations and value their achievements. It helps enormously when nursery staff are flexible about their provision and able to think about individual children's needs.

Adult-led activities are best used sparingly for children under three. The children will benefit much more from adult attention and support as they pursue their own preoccupations. Providing open-ended play materials, and protected time for children to explore them, fosters rich and varied playing and learning.

> **QUESTIONS FOR REFLECTION**
>
> ● How are play materials chosen for your nursery?
> ● How are they organised and made available to the children?
> ● Thinking of a child you know well, what does he enjoy playing with most? What else could you offer to feed his interest?
> ● How could you broaden the range of play materials in your nursery to reflect a wide range of cultures?
> ● How can you maximise the learning opportunities in the nursery environment as a whole?

4. Adult reflection and learning

The entire framework in this book is offered to support reflection and staff development. The extent to which staff can develop a reflective approach to their practice depends not only upon individuals' abilities and experience, but also upon the quality of the ongoing support they receive from their managers.

A key area of support is training, both initial and ongoing. Nursery staff are generally warm and committed to the children in their care, but good instincts are not enough. In order to respond to the needs of the children skilfully, imaginatively and consistently, staff need a secure knowledge of how children develop, learn and think, time and space to observe individual children and opportunities to explore their thoughts and reactions with others in one-to-one and team meetings.

At the moment, daycare practitioners, except those in senior positions, may not even have initial training, and many are relatively young and inexperienced. In the study on which this book is based, less than half the staff interviewed – all of whom were working with children under three – had completed any formal training.

Above all, it helps children's learning and well-being when staff themselves have a healthy disposition to learn. Some people, managers and staff alike, may feel uncomfortably challenged by some elements of the framework, with its emphasis on the need to respond to individual children's needs, on the importance of children's intellectual development and on supporting attachment. Practitioners need support to become comfortable with working in a continual cycle of planning, doing and reviewing – to use the High/Scope* phrase – and with being lifelong learners.

The confidence which comes with appropriate training and support, and the perception of oneself as a lifelong learner, greatly helps staff to form positive relationships with other practitioners and, crucially, with parents, enabling them to work in partnership.

Rachel

'When Julie comes to do her observation of me, well, it was a bit scary at first. But she is so supportive and it is really good to be able to talk about how I am doing with her afterwards. It is impossible to see yourself from the outside, isn't it? She says what she is doing is 'holding up the mirror'. She noticed how well I was responding to Rosie – having a conversation with her, getting eye contact and answering her little gestures and noises. I know that's really important for her learning how to talk and for her feeling good about herself.'

4.1 Adults take time to observe, reflect and revise their practice in a continuous cycle

It helps when staff are encouraged and supported to reflect upon their own practice, learning from what has gone well and from the occasional disaster. Working with young children is often challenging as well as rewarding; reflection helps practitioners to digest experience and share with others what they have learned.

Reflection, particularly written reflection, widens the possibilities of learning from each other and of mutual support. It also supports the development of professional objectivity. It can be used in a number of different contexts: individual reflection, with a manager, with the larger team. Staff can share difficulties, celebrate successes and pool their knowledge of individual children. They can record any concerns or examples of good practice that can be shared.

When staff reflect like this upon their own practice, it enables more focused discussion with line managers. Self-evaluation can play an important part in staff support and monitoring, complementing the line manager's own observations of individual practice. This kind of monitoring is much more productive if undertaken supportively, sharing observations and thoughts and building on the positive. It may well highlight training and development needs, which can then be incorporated into training plans. As well as managers observing the practice of staff, staff may welcome carefully-managed peer observation and feedback.

It helps when staff consider together what kind of structures would best support their reflective learning. They may like to think about what forms observation and reflection should take, the frequency and format of monitoring sessions and how best to share observation and reflection within the team.

Another key area of observation in a nursery is observation of children. Being able to step back in a busy nursery and see what is happening, even for five minutes, offers a very different perspective from being in the thick of it. Observing a child closely is as near as an adult can get to understanding what is going on in his head. Staff need training and support to develop their observation skills in relation to children and – just as important – freed-up time in which to do it. Sharing observations of children with their parents can greatly support working in partnership, offering a chance for staff and parents to pool their knowledge.

All this observation, reflection and revision of practice is often known in shorthand as 'reflective practice'. It takes time, but it is time well spent, as this is an area with enormous potential to raise the quality of the care given. The point is to improve practice and meet the children's needs better: reflection is recycled back into practice through supervision, planning, organisation and provision. Once there is a continuous cycle of planning, doing and reviewing, it means that practitioners are comfortable – even enthusiastic – about being continual learners. This often leads to greater job satisfaction.

KEYPOINTS

- When staff reflect upon their own practice, the quality is greatly enhanced.
- Self-evaluation complements observation by others.
- A continuous cycle of planning, doing and reviewing has great potential to raise both quality and job satisfaction.

Rachel

'Doing the modules from the Early Childhood Studies course has been a big thing for me. I didn't do A levels at school and the idea of seminars and having to do assignments was pretty scary. But we go to college on a Monday morning and the course has been really interesting and explained a lot about why we do the things we do at nursery. I was dead nervous when we had to do a

4.2 Adults are given and make good use of opportunities for accredited learning

There are many reasons to offer staff opportunities for accredited learning. In order to offer high-quality care, practitioners need high-quality initial and in-service training, particularly in the interrelated areas of child development, young children's learning and thinking and observation of children.

Accredited learning offers powerful recognition to the learner, which raises self-esteem and provides motivation to further learning. It enhances motivation presentation – but it was over in a flash and everyone said it was really good! when I have finished the year I will have credit points which mean I have done part of a degree.'

and confidence generally and it opens up possibilities for career development. Accredited learning is particularly effective in valuing the learner and the learning.

Accredited learning also contributes to raising the status of caring for young children and gives the lie to the widely-held assumption that, the younger the children someone works with, the fewer qualifications and abilities are needed. In 2000 Early Education (The British Association for Early Childhood Education) adopted a resolution that, while welcoming the growing investment in the care and education of young children across the UK, members recommended that national standards for childcare should aspire to a minimum of Level 3 NVQ/SVQ appropriate qualifications over time. This may be seen as an entitlement for both children and the adults charged to care for them.

Accredited learning is one of many opportunities for learning and development. Other opportunities include:
- reflective practice and learning from the job
- supervision
- coaching/mentoring
- shadowing
- reading
- internal and external training which is not accredited
- visits to other settings.

KEYPOINTS

- Accredited learning values both the learning and the learner.
- It also contributes to raising the status of caring for young children.
- There are many other opportunities for learning and development too.

Rachel

'As well as putting the older children's paintings up on the wall, we also take photos of things they have made or the things they are doing. We had a really funny one of five children hiding in the cardboard box the washing machine came in. I noticed Ollie staring at the photo. He looked at me, pointed at the picture and said, "That's me and Tamara. *We* did that!"'

Rachel

'I was having a hard time opening a parcel covered in Sellotape, and Finn was watching me. I said, "I'm having a struggle here, but I'll manage in the end". Later on I saw Finn having a hard time trying to fit two bits of Brio track together (he had them the wrong way round). I swear I heard him say to himself something like, "I'm having a struggle, but I'll manage!" He did, too.'

4.3 Adults model positive learning dispositions

Children would appear to be born with the full set of positive learning dispositions*, but by the time some children reach primary school, the flame has already gone out. Sadly, they have been 'turned off' learning and do not see themselves as learners.

As children's attitudes are strongly influenced by those adults who care for them, adults are in a strong position to nurture positive learning dispositions which go deep enough to stay with a child into adulthood. Positive learning dispositions include: concentrating, persisting, exploring, experimenting, reflecting, questioning and forming hypotheses. These tendencies are evidence of how positively someone feels about learning and how they see themselves in relation to it.

As we have seen in other aspects of the framework, modelling is a powerful tool for learning. It helps children when they see adults concentrating on a difficult task or struggling with something but persisting and being proud of success in the end. It helps them when adults celebrate their own achievements, for instance, by displaying their certificates of achievement. It helps children to see adults experimenting and puzzling things out. It can be useful for adults to think out loud in such a situation, for the benefit of the children, for example, 'I wonder why this blind isn't working today? Let's take a look'.

'Wondering why' is important. Even tiny babies are capable of forming hypotheses and testing them out and, with the support of adults who recognise that, they will continue to develop as curious, persistent learners, determined to pursue their questions.

KEYPOINTS

- Modelling is a powerful tool for learning.
- It helps when adults model positive learning dispositions.
- Positive learning dispositions include: persisting, experimenting, wondering and questioning.

Conclusion

When staff are supported to develop the attitudes known collectively as 'reflective learning', there is no limit to their potential development as practitioners. When they model them to the children they care for, they are fostering something very valuable, which may stay with the children for their lifetime of learning.

QUESTIONS FOR REFLECTION

- How is adult reflection and learning supported in your nursery?
- Are you aware of your own training and development needs?
- Do you have opportunities for accredited learning?
- How do you model positive learning dispositions to the children?

GLOSSARY

These words appear with an asterisk in the text.

Attachment

In this context, an affectionate bond between a child and an adult, characterised by reciprocity and a sense of commitment. The relationship offers a young child the feeling of belonging, reliability and security.

High/Scope

The High/Scope programme, initially known as the Perry Pre-school Project, is a North American pre-school intervention programme, involving training for staff in settings and parental involvement. Subject to long-term research, it has been shown to have lasting positive results for children as they grow into adulthood, both educationally and socially. An important aspect of the programme is to introduce young children to the idea of planning what they would like to do, doing it and then reflecting, often in a group, on how it went and what they would like to do next.

Key person approach

An approach in which each child (and his family) has someone in the nursery with whom they have a special relationship, a relationship of attachment. A key person differs from a key worker, in that while the role includes elements of organisation and coordination, the focus is the relationship itself, and the benefits it brings. See Elfer, Goldschmied and Selleck (2002).

Learning dispositions

Positive learning dispositions are attitudes and tendencies in children and adults which support learning. They include: curiosity, concentration, persistence and willingness to explore, reflect, question and form hypotheses. See Roberts (2002) and Peers Early Education Partnership (2000).

Scaffolding

Structuring, supporting and extending children's learning experiences, initially providing a lot of support and intervention, but gradually taking down the 'scaffolding' as the child is able to progress more independently. This idea was developed by Jerome Bruner and others from the work of Lev Vygotsky.

Schemas

Schemas, sometimes called play patterns, are patterns of repeatable behaviour which reflect and support children's developing thought . Originally arising from the insights of the Swiss psychologist, Jean Piaget, they are thought to play a key role in children's cognitive development, becoming gradually more complex and used in combination. For instance, repeated experience of throwing a ball (trajectory schema) leads on to the development of complex concepts of distance and speed. Common schemas for children under three include: rotation, trajectory, enclosure, connection and transportation. See Nutbrown (1994) and Peers Early Education Partnership (2000), *Learning together with Ones: Play Patterns*, *Learning together with Threes: Making the Most of Play Patterns*.

Treasure basket

A basket of objects for babies to explore, sometimes themed, sometimes with a mix of objects. Babies are offered a variety of shapes and textures and objects which are man-made and natural. They can enjoy the basket either on their own or with other babies, but always with an interested adult nearby, to support their independent explorations. See Goldschmied (2000).

Vygotsky

Lev Vygotsky (1896–1934) was a Russian psychologist who developed a theory of child development which emphasises the role of the society and culture in which a child is growing up and therefore the adult role in children's learning. He developed the idea of the 'zone of proximal development', or what the child can nearly do, which is where an adult can be most helpful.

SUGGESTED READING

Core reading

Brown, B (1998) *Unlearning Discrimination in the Early Years.* Trentham Books

Bruce, T (2001) *Learning through Play: Babies, toddlers and the foundation years.* Hodder & Stoughton

Early Years Trainers Anti-Racist Network (1999) *All Our Children: a guide for those who care*

Elfer, P, Goldschmied, E and Selleck, D (2002) *Key Persons in Nurseries.* National Early Years Network

Goldschmied, E (2000) *Infants at Work: Babies of 6–9 months exploring everyday objects* (Video) National Children's Bureau. London

Leach, P (1997) *Your Baby and Child.* Penguin Books

Purves, L and Selleck, D (1999) *Tuning into Children.* BBC Education

Roberts, R (2002) *Self-esteem and Successful Early Learning.* Paul Chapman

Peers Early Education Partnership (2000) *Learning Together* (a series of folders, song-tapes and videos). PEEP

Whalley, M (1997) *Working with Parents,* especially Chapter 3, 'Sharing ideas with Parents about How Children Learn'. Hodder & Stoughton

Further reading and viewing

Baby it's You (1994) Channel 4 video

Dowling, M (2000) *Young Children's Personal, Social and Emotional Development.* Paul Chapman

Goldschmied, E and Jackson, S (1994) *People Under Three.* Routledge

Goldschmied, E and Selleck, D (1996) *Communication between Babies in their First Year.* National Children's Bureau

Gopnik, A, Meltzoff, A and Kuhl, P (1999) *How Babies Think.* Phoenix

Nutbrown, C (1994) *Threads of Thinking.* Paul Chapman

Trevarthen, C 'The child's need to learn a culture', *Children and Society, 9,1*

INDEX